Mosquito

The Wooden Wonder

4th Edition

Edward Bishop

Airlife
England

4th edition published in the UK in 2000
by Airlife Publishing Ltd

1st Edition published in 1959 by Max Parish & Co. Ltd.
2nd Edition published in 1980 by Airlife Publishing Ltd
3rd Edition published in 1995 by Airlife Publishing Ltd

British Library Cataloguing-in-Publication Data
   A catalogue record for this book
   is available from the British Library

ISBN 1 84037 212 5

Printed and bound in Great Britain by
Butler & Tanner Ltd, Frome and London

Airlife Publishing Ltd

101 Longden Road, Shrewsbury, SY3 9EB, England
E-mail: airlife@airlifebooks.com
Website: www.airlifebooks.com

Contents

Acknowledgements

It is more than fifty years since Sir Geoffrey de Havilland first, and unsuccessfully, suggested a fast wooden unarmed bomber to the Air Ministry.

I am indebted therefore to Sir Geoffrey, Major Hereward de Havilland, DSO, Mr C. C. Walker, CBE, Mr R. E. Bishop, CBE — not related to me — Mr C. T. Wilkins, OBE, Mr W. A. Tamblin and their colleagues of the de Havilland Aircraft Company Limited for thinking back from the days of space to more leisured times when 400 m.p.h. was considered an astonishing (if not impossible) speed for a bomber.

I am indebted also to Air Marshal Sir Geoffrey Tuttle, KBE, CB, DFC, formerly Deputy Chief of the Air Staff, for his personal interest in this project from the start, and to Elizabeth, Lady Freeman for her encouragement and most helpful introductions.

At the Air Historical Branch of the Air Ministry I received most courteous assistance, which was inaugurated by Mr J. C. Nerney, ISO, and carried on by Mr L. A. Jackets whose colleagues Mr R. O. Ward, Mr W. H. Martin and Mr D. C. Bateman would often reappear from the archives dusty yet triumphant. As on the day Mr Bateman discovered a fading photograph of Vicky the Bear that flew with No. 89 Squadron. At the Information Division Mr 'Chris' Cole's sustained enthusiasm was a constant source of inspiration.

The most memorable part of writing this story was the pleasure with which Service and civilian people who were associated with the Mosquito welcomed my enquiries. The sentiment behind their co-operation is, I think, best reflected in these words from Group Captain F. L. Dodd, DSO, DFC, AFC: 'I was delighted to hear that at last somebody is going to do justice to the Mosquito, for it certainly was a magnificent aeroplane — almost certainly the best all-round performer ever produced by any country.'

Finally, my acknowledgement would not be complete without the expression of a slender hope that all those who hold special memories of the Mosquito will feel that due justice has been done.

E.B.

Chapter 1
Prologue

On 30th January 1943, the tenth anniversary of Hitler's seizure of power, Reichsmarshal Goering was scheduled to address a large assembly of the Wehrmacht at the German Air Ministry at 11 a.m.

A few moments before eleven o'clock, German radio listeners heard an announcer say, 'A dignified ceremony of a military character is taking place in the Hall of Honour at the Reich Air Ministry'. Then Berlin went off the air.

The Mosquito, the RAF's 'wooden wonder', had arrived to join the party.

Sweeping across the city at 350 m.p.h. three crack crews from No. 105 Squadron, led by Squadron Leader R. W. Reynolds and Pilot Officer E. B.

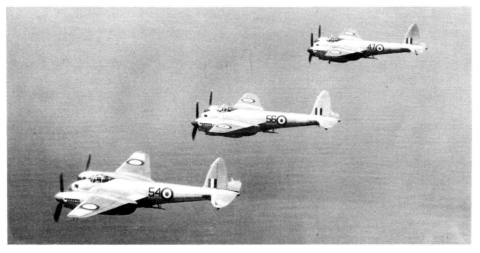

Seen here in the early 1960s are three Mosquitos of 3 CAACU. They are (from camera) VP191, TA719 and RS709. The latter two still survive today. *(Harry Ellis)*

Sismore, dropped their bombs and returned safely — none being more pleased to do so than Flight Lieutenant J. Gordon and his navigator, Flying Officer R. G. Hayes, who only three days earlier had caught their port wing in some telegraph wires on a low-level mission.

At 4 p.m. Goebbels, the Nazi propaganda chief, had arranged to make a follow-up speech in Berlin. On the dot, the Mosquitos returned. Flying at a low level across the North Sea to a point north of Heligoland, this formation turned inland at Lübeck. Fifty miles from Berlin, the Mosquitos began their climb 'off the deck' to a height of 20,000 feet, until the capital appeared below them in brilliant winter sunshine. Squadron Leader D. F. W. Darling, who led this second attack, and his navigator, Flying Officer W. Wright, failed to return.

Twice in a day, and for the first time in the war, Berlin was bombed in broad daylight. Both attacks were pressed home in circumstances which appealed enormously to the British sense of humour. For Hermann Goering, whose Luftwaffe had failed to intercept the Mosquitos, had, in a way, himself stage-managed the RAF's daring performance. From then on the Mosquito, and the men who flew in her, had a moral superiority over the Luftwaffe — and they never lost it.

Fifteen years later, I pushed through the plate-glass doors of the building in Whitehall which then housed the Air Ministry and the Board of Trade.

'Ah, yes, Mosquitos,' said the man at the door, knowledgeably. 'Come to talk about Mosquitos. This way, sir.'

Before I could amplify my appointment I was escorted to a kindly person behind a reception desk. She speedily involved herself in a number of telephone enquiries, then returned to me with a puzzled expression on her face.

'Frankly,' she said, 'I am not sure who to put you on to. It's — well, it's rather an unusual request.'

I smiled, and agreed that perhaps, as it all happened rather a long time ago . . . .

She cut me off. 'It would help,' she said in an official tone, 'if you could tell me whether they are for export or import, and of what species.'

'But this *is* the Air Ministry, isn't it?' I asked.

Gusts of the most unbusinesslike laughter on both sides of a very solid Board of Trade counter led me to believe that I had said something foolish. Somehow this seemed an appropriate beginning for the story of the aircraft nicknamed in Whitehall, 'Freeman's Folly'.

Chapter 2
Where the Mosquito Was Born

'I live in a free house,' said W. J. ('Oliver') Goldsmith, wartime Captain of Marines.

'Oh?' said I. 'Keep a pub, do you?' It seemed quite a sensible question, amid the cocktail chatter at a party given by Peter Dimmock of the BBC.

'No. It's a sort of stately home really.'

The house was free, he explained, because it was a scheduled ancient monument, under the care of the Ministry of Works. And another point of interest about it was that the Mosquito aircraft had been designed in the ballroom, and the prototype was built on the cabbage patch.

'Actually,' he went on, 'I have just pulled the ballroom down, but Bishop, the de Havilland chief designer, did all his work in the manorial hall!' Oliver Goldsmith looked at me sharply. 'I don't think you believe a word of this,' he said. 'Why not come down to dinner this weekend, and let me show you round? Salisbury Hall's the name of the place. Near St Albans. A turning off the London-Birmingham road — can't miss it. Can't miss the house either. There's a moat, you know.'

I duly dined with the Goldsmiths that weekend, and as the soft yellow candlelight threw our twentieth-century shadows across the black-and-white chequered stone floor. Oliver's wife, Audrey, told me how they had come to Salisbury Hall.

'We decided we wanted to live in the country. So, one weekend when Oliver was playing cricket near here, he packed me off with a large-scale map on which he had marked the likely places where I might come across some old barracks of falling-down houses.

'Well, I reached Salisbury Hall at the end of a very hot day and I must admit I said to myself that no one could ever live here. The house was derelict, the garden a jungle and the moat a mass of weed. I drove back to the cricket match, and by the time Oliver had been bowled out, I felt I ought to show him that I hadn't been wasting my time.

'Later on, after we had made up our minds to go mad and take the house, we discovered that it was officially an ancient monument. Oliver went to see some people at the Ministry of Works, and they seemed delighted to find somebody crazy enough to want to live here.'

The Goldsmiths moved in, camped in two rooms, and slaved to make Salisbury Hall inhabitable. Indoors they dusted the cobwebs off a number of mysterious 'No Smoking' notices. Outdoors, scything down the long grass, they stumbled into five deep and roomy air-raid shelters. They also cleaned the flint-lined moat which yielded the first of a number of surprises. The mass of weed clogging the waterway was *Elodea canadensis*, much in demand, by aquarists. Oliver Goldsmith swapped a load of it for a stock of goldfish.

The candles burned low, our shadows mixing incongruously with that of a suit of armour which stood stiffly over us. We talked into the night until the dull Tudor table pewter, which Marine frogmen had salvaged from the moat, was scarcely discernible.

I asked about the history of the house and learned that here in this room King Charles II had supped with Nell Gwynne who lodged in the little cottage by the moat. And here 'pretty, witty' Nell is said to have held their son over the moat, threatening to drop him in unless Charles ennobled him. But just in time the King had cried, 'Don't drown the Duke of St Albans!'

'Nell haunts the place too,' Oliver said, 'But you don't see her, only hear her.'

'Oh, what do you hear?'

'The creaking of the old four-poster bed. Used to disturb the de Havilland people back in 1940, when they were fire-watching.'

Flukish chance had brought the Goldsmiths to Salisbury Hall, but in what circumstances had the creators of the DH98, the ninety-eighth de Havilland design, come here? Why build an aeroplane in an old barrack like this when all the facilities of the de Havilland headquarters at Hatfield were only five miles away?

Musing in the afterglow of a good dinner, I wondered if, in one marvellously impulsive moment, the business men of the aircraft company had been seized by the romance of building a modern bomber behind a mediaeval moat.

Some days later, when I learned the hard practical reasons which brought Bishop and his colleagues from Hatfield to Salisbury Hall, I reflected that it was perhaps a blessing that history had not been taken into account. In the days of Edward the Confessor, the manor belonged to one Asgar the Staller — a name to put off the doughtiest of aircraft designers.

Sir Geoffrey de Havilland, tall and lean, stretched back in an armchair, and passed his long, tapering fingers across his brow. In the distance, even with the windows closed, one could hear the muffled roar of the engine tests for the new Comet 4. As he transported his thoughts back to the beginning of the Mosquito story, Sir Geoffrey turned his head towards his old friend and colleague, Mr C. C. Walker.

'It's so long ago it's difficult to remember, isn't it?'

It was in the autumn of 1938, in the critical days of Munich, that de Havilland and Walker tried to interest the authorities in their idea for a twin-engined, high-speed, unarmed wooden bomber. They went up together to the Air Ministry, and spoke 'on a high level', but all they got was a tentative suggestion that they should build a wing for somebody else's aeroplane. 'It was to be called the Ape, I believe,' said Walker with a chuckle.

Very little Government contract work had been placed with de Havilland since 1919. The official thinking behind this offer was to give the company an opportunity to accustom itself to the paper work involved.

'CRISIS — LATEST' stared at them menacingly from the placards as de Havilland and Walker, two disheartened men, drove back to Hatfield. On the road de Havilland turned to Walker and said, 'We'll do it anyway.'

'You know', Sir Geoffrey said to me, 'Freeman is really the chap you ought to find out about first.'

Freeman. Sir Geoffrey had spoken the key word in the Mosquito story, Air Marshal Sir Wilfrid Rhodes Freeman, the man who, as Air Member of the Air Council for Development and Production, had insisted on ordering — in the face of opposition — the first 50 Mosquitos, was the point where the story must begin.

'If there had been a Freeman between the wars,' said de Havilland, 'the whole picture of our air strength might have been very different. Do you know what I mean by a commonsense man? Well, Wilfrid Freeman was a commonsense man. Unfortunately, such men only come to the top when it's a question of the nation's survival.

'I first met him in France early in the first war. He went there with No. 2 Squadron. I remember that he was greatly impressed during that war by the performance of the DH4. He was affected by his personal experience of flying a bomber as fast as a fighter — and that, of course, was always our conception for the aeroplane which was to become the Mosquito.'

He dug out a back number of the *de Havilland Gazette* and showed me a marked paragraph:

> Had it not been for the support and encouragement of Sir Wilfrid Freeman . . . the Mosquito would probably not have materialized.

5

The DH4 — the high speed bomber of World War I. *(IWM)*

He stressed its value for reconnaissance. The project was known as 'Freeman's Folly' and there was no general interest in it outside Hatfield.

Wilfrid Freeman served his country in the second world war from behind a desk. He did not dwell in the headlines; he disliked publicity. This made my search for information about him no easier, but there was this tribute from Lord Beaverbrook in 1942: 'More than any single man, Sir Wilfrid Freeman has provided the RAF with aeroplanes whose superiority over the enemy has been proved in battle.' This was praise indeed, coming from the man who has himself received so much acclaim for this work as Minister of Aircraft Production from Dunkirk until after the Battle of Britain. And Marshal of the RAF Sir John Slessor, in his autobiography, quotes a telling letter from Lord Hives of Rolls-Royce:

> It was the expansion which was carried out under Wilfrid's direction in 1937 to 1939 which enabled the Battle of Britain to be won. Without that foresight and imagination no efforts in 1940 would have yielded any results.[1]

A tribute which, as Sir John writes in his book, came from a man who was in a position to know better than most people what he was talking about.

I went down to Chichester at the invitation of Elizabeth, Lady Freeman, Sir Wilfrid's widow. Lunch was served at a table which stood beneath a large oil painting of Wilfrid Rhodes Freeman in the uniform of an Air Chief Marshal. The room was also lined with his books, among

[1] *The Central Blue* (Cassell).

6

them a set of Spenser of which the first volume is inscribed:

'To Wilfrid Freeman, who did more than any other man to build up and maintain the strength and quality of the Royal Air Force during the most critical years of our country's history from 1939-45, these volumes are represented as a sincere and affectionate token of gratitude for his inspiring friendship and collaboration' — R. Stafford Cripps.

That day, and during later visits to Lady Freeman's home, the portrait on the dining-room wall dominated me.

I studied closely the gritty determination in the eyes, the lips and the jaw; an expression that epitomized the dauntless character of this Presbyterian Scot who, placing quality before quantity, worked loyally but unharmoniously at the Ministry of Aircraft Production during the Battle of Britain with that other, more tempestuous Presbyterian, Lord Beaverbrook. Here was the man who, as Lord Portal had told me, 'never afraid to take the unpopular course', insisted on de Havilland's fast unarmed wooden bomber against very great opposition, when others thought it was too late in the day to consider the Mosquito.

To quote a BBC Battle of Britain anniversary broadcast by Sir John Slessor, shortly after Freeman's death in 1953, 'Some of his most important and fruitful decisions, such as to order the Mosquito or go ahead with Whittle's jet, were taken against formidable technical advice, and involved running real risks.'

Below the head in this portrait my eyes met a black tie, knotted conventionally into the soft, woollen, collar-attached non-regulation shirt which advertised the individuality of an airman who never succumbed to the uniformity of the service; the very last man of whom it could be said that he was a 'Raf type'.

I looked for his service cap. It was not in the portrait. A pity. This headgear, I had learned from Lord Portal, also conformed to Freeman's almost studied non-conformity. It was no regulation 'brass hat'. The Air Chief Marshal had designed it for himself, directing that the gold leaves be stitched to the plain blue cloth peak of a more junior officer's cap. Ordinarily they would be backed by black leather.

Lower, where the brass buttons of his Air Force blue tunic began, the top button was left undone — symbolic reminder that Wilfrid Freeman first went to war in 1914 as a fighter pilot with No. 2 Squadron. Later he flew the DH4, the combination between a de Havilland design and a Rolls-Royce engine which was the Mosquito of its day.

Even the belt below the buttons is awry in the painting, twisted out of alignment by Freeman's thumb which is latched on to the blue material, as he sits in an attitude that captures two of his chief characteristics — an inability to suffer fools gladly, and deep contemplation of a problem.

Just such a problem, for instance, as the Mosquito, which, started on 'spec', was in late 1939 already appearing in some detail on the de Havilland drawing-boards in the ballroom of Salisbury Hall.

Chapter 3
Ordered Off the Drawing-Board

In the months that followed Captain de Havilland's patriotic decision to 'do it anyway', the plan for the unarmed wooden speed bomber had become partly submerged in the tide of events. By 3rd September 1939, when Britain declared war on Germany, Hatfield was producing Oxford twin-engined trainers to augment Airspeed's output at Christchurch, as well as Tiger Moth trainers, Queen Bees, Moth Minors and a few Flamingos, a transport type in which King George VI made many wartime inspection flights.

Apart from the personal encouragement which de Havilland was receiving from Wilfrid Freeman for this 'private venture' aeroplane, the conception of a rakish twin-engine wooden warplane which would bomb Berlin in daylight was still not received with any enthusiasm by the Air Staff. There was opposition to 'Freeman's Folly' on the grounds that it was too late to think about new designs for *this* war. It would be wrong, it was argued, to divert skilled effort to an aeroplane which had not even been officially ordered. It would be doubly wrong to spend time and labour on a wooden aircraft, for military aircraft were now constructed of metal. It was known that the Luftwaffe had experimented with laminated wood and dropped it.

In this climate de Havilland decided that speed in the design and building of a prototype Mosquito was as essential to the survival of the idea as its speed on the clock, once it became operational, would be to the survival of the aircraft itself. Pace of the work on the prototype would depend on peace for the design team. No one knew this better than Bishop.[1] Once before the detachment of a de Havilland design team to a haven of peace had paid off. That was in the summer of 1927, six years after Bishop joined the company as its second premium apprentice. Then, in ten weeks, a team working in a couple of attics in Fishermen's

[1] R. E. Bishop, then Chief Designer, later Deputy Managing Director.

Walk, near Bournemouth, had given birth to the DH61, a big single-engined biplane.

So Bishop and his colleague R. M. Clarkson, the Company's chief aerodynamicist,[1] had called on Rumball & Edwards, house agents of St Albans, and Salisbury Hall was one of six suggestions.

Bishop was 'sold' on Salisbury Hall for practical rather than aesthetic reasons. While he admired the rose brick rising solidly from the Roman mound, he had to concern himself with the cubic capacity, ancient or modern, that it contained. The rooms, though rather dark, were large, and there was a lofty Edwardian ballroom which might have been built for his draughtsmen. Compared with the attics of Fishermen's Walk, Salisbury Hall was a palace. Bishop and his team moved into the old house and very soon the moat was encircling a self-contained 'cottage industry' unique in the story of aviation.

Tim Wilkins, who was a young member of Bishop's 'first eleven',[2] retains one vivid memory of the beginning of the Mosquito at Salisbury Hall.

'There was a stuffed pike in a glass case on the wall of the lavatory', he recalls, adding lightly, 'It is just possible the lines of that fish had some influence on the shape of the fuselage of the Mosquito.'

Whether or not one cares to give credence to this amusing thought, the fact remains that the fish was already a Very Important Pike. Winston Churchill had caught it in the moat when visiting his mother who lived at Salisbury Hall before the first war.

With or without the inspiration of Churchill's catch, Bishop set up his drawing-board on the chequered floor of the manorial hall. He took a thick black pencil and outlined a sleek, clean, twin-engine monoplane. Now, that may read as a preposterous piece of over-simplification. But an aeroplane has to start somewhere. It cannot begin as a detailed drawing. Somebody must give a lead, and that is the duty of the Chief Designer.

Ordinarily, there would follow a series of stages from the first rough thick pencil lay-out, through harder and harder pencils, as the drawing becomes more accurate. With the Mosquito the pressure was on. Often the production people were to sweat blood translating freehand drawings into aircraft components.

There were not only months to make up, but years. The mother of the Mosquito had flown in 1934 — the Comet Racer, which at this moment, as Bishop and his team set to work, was parked under a tarpaulin on the edge of Gravesend airfield like so much junk.

The Comet Racer was a most advanced aeroplane in its day. It emerged

[1] Later Research Director.

[2] C. T. Wilkins, then de Havilland's Assistant Chief Designer, later Design Director.

The hangar at Salisbury Hall, where the prototype Mosquito was built. *(British Aerospace)*

Work in progress inside the hangar. *(British Aerospace)*

The DH Comet Racer, whose sleek lines influenced the design of the Mosquito.

under the spur of competition for a £10,000 Mildenhall to Melbourne first prize put up by Sir McPherson Robertson, an Australian chocolate maker.

Crewed by C. W. A. Scott and T. Campbell Black, it won the famous England to Australia air race. With a pair of Gipsy Six 225 h.p. racing engines it was the first aircraft to achieve a range exceeding 2,800 miles at a speed of 225 m.p.h. under Certificate of Airworthiness conditions. It was also the first British aircraft to combine the three most modern devices of the time — retractable undercarriage, wing flaps and variable-pitch propellers.

Compare the Comet Racer and the Mosquito of 1940 and there is a strong family resemblance. But in 1934 the British Government showed less interest in its performance than the French and the Portuguese Air Forces, both of which subsequently bought the other two Comets entered in the race. G-ACSS, the winner, was investigated by the Air Ministry and thrown back into the pond of pre-war civil flying — an odd fish out.

But the Comet Racer continued its career privately, making record after record, until finally in March 1938, piloted by A. E. Clouston and Victor Ricketts, it was flown from England to New Zealand and back — more than 26,000 miles — in eleven days.

The Comet and other pre-natal circumstances combined to influence Bishop as he worked on the first Mosquito. Bishop had learned his craft under Arthur Hagg, who designed the Comet Racer. Hagg was an aircraft designer by profession and a boat builder by hobby. (Today he is in business on his own account as a professional boat builder.) He introduced at least one boat-building feature into the Comet Racer. He planked the wing with spruce strips, the strips of one layer crossing those of another layer at approximately right angles.

When Arthur Hagg left the company, Bishop took charge of the design office and became responsible for the Albatross four-engine wooden airliner, which might be termed the Maiden Aunt of the Mosquito. Certainly the Albatross formed another segment of the experience which Bishop brought to the Mosquito.

In addition, with no time for special research, the speedy creation of the Mosquito was assisted by everything de Havilland and Rolls-Royce had learned from World War I onwards.

Bishop's move to the old house paid off. The divorce of his design team from the production hubbub at Hatfield was producing the desired effect. Distractions at Salisbury Hall were minor or amusing. There was the day, during the 'phoney war', when the men at their drawing-boards, hearing the sound of a huntsman's horn, dashed into the garden and saw a pink-coated hunt galloping across the meadow beyond the

Under construction — a new home for the de Havilland Museum Trust's collection of historic aircraft at Salisbury Hall. *(Philip J. Birtles)*

moat. And at night there was also, of course, Nell Gwynne. 'We never saw her,' Rex King, then Assistant Experimental Manager, recalls, 'but my word, did that creaking four-poster keep the fire-watchers awake!'

Very soon the first mock-up took shape. It was suspended, like some grotesque carcase, from the ceiling of the kitchen, which being vast and old-fashioned, provided space for a number of activities. The production men worked at the far end until their shop was ready. The switchboard girl sat in her earphone harness at the near end. And the cooking area functioned under the command of Bishop's secretary, Mrs Ledeboer, who supervised the catering.

The first Christmas of the war brought great excitement to the civilians at Salisbury Hall, and a rewarding moment for de Havilland. The 'private venture' aeroplane, that mock-up Mosquito hanging from the roof of the kitchen, became official. A letter from Freeman specified the new aeroplane as the B1/40. He ordered fifty of them — fifty fast wooden reconnaissance bombers.

Wilfrid Freeman had won for his 'Folly' the rarest of Government concessions. It was an order 'off the drawing-board'.

England came out of that bleak winter into the spring of 1940. In Europe good campaigning weather was on the way, and Hitler poised his Panzers for the Blitzkrieg. At Salisbury Hall a first crocus appeared on the lawn by the moat, and drawings multiplied. The aeroplane developed.

Spring also brought the Brass Hats from the Air Ministry — among them Tedder, to express his thoughts on the B1/40 in lightning doodle sketches. Bishop was none too happy about the awakening of official interest at the top. While Spec. B1/40 dangled a little ludicrously from the ceiling of the kitchen and remained 'Freeman's Folly', he knew that his clean, immaculate conception could not be despoiled. Once Brass Hats began to descend on his moated retreat, Bishop feared interference. This fear was borne out. Fussation followed official recognition.

Up shot the old bogey of armament. Bishop and his team groaned at official suggestions. They were building a speed bomber, to race in, bomb and retire at a speed which would give enemy fighters a run for their money. And now here was the Air Ministry asking, why not put in a gun turret and a third crew member?

At this point, another aspect of their task was bothering de Havilland. They were building a fast, unarmed bomber, but how great would the bomb load be? When Captain de Havilland and Mr Walker first mooted the speed bomber in 1938 they suggested a load of four 250-lb. bombs. At peace in 1938 this bomb load had seemed impressive. In 1940, in the anger of war, it presented a new challenge.

Bishop and his team studied the standard 250-lb. bomb and decided that the tail fin was occupying too much space and wasting weight. Bombs were not de Havilland business, but they began to consider the

Mrs B. A. Hale formed a 'cottage industry' group with her neighbours to make Mosquito parts in a hut in her Welwyn garden — a novel kind of dispersal of industry, in which many others like her played their part.

problem. Bishop said, 'Why not cut the fin down or damned nearly off altogether?' They did. They tested the sawn-off bomb by dropping it on their own airfield at Hatfield. It worked. The new speed bomber's payload was doubled in a throw and a first step had been taken towards the time when Mosquito bombers would carry 4,000-pounders.

And then came another bombshell. Lord Beaverbrook, appointed after Dunkirk as the first Minister of Aircraft Production in the new Churchill Government, sent out a directive.

Stop work on the Mosquito, he ordered.

In this critical summer of 1940, when at any moment Britain expected to hear invasion bells ringing out from every parish church, pikes were issued to the Home Guard and tommy-guns to the warriors of Whitehall. Air Marshal Sir Wilfrid Freeman kept a tommy-gun in the office and it was jocularly feared that he would shoot Lord Beaverbrook if the Minister did not very soon reinstate the Mosquito.

In July, Beaverbrook relented. The Mosquito was 'on' again. Beaverbrook lived, and in place of one quick burst of fire, Freeman let off steam to his wife about the Beaver.

But Beaverbrook soon appreciated the special advantages of 'Freeman's Folly'. The new aeroplane was made of wood. It would make few calls on the forging and other metal industries for men or materials. With the Luftwaffe seeking to destroy our aircraft industry, its method of construction lent itself to the all-important requirement of dispersal. And soon indeed, housewives were to make Mosquito parts in their kitchens and backyards — like Mrs B. A. Hale, who formed a group of neighbours to work at her home in Welwyn. The enemy would be hard put to hunt down and bomb a hundred Mrs Hales.

In the meantime Harry Povey, the de Havilland production wizard, had rounded up the furniture firms, many of whose skilled men were put out of work by the war. Modern furniture would not suit Salisbury Hall, where Oliver Goldsmith now sleeps in Nell Gwynne's four-poster, but a combination of some of the raw materials used in its manufacture, and the craftsmanship which makes bedroom suites for ideal homes, would build you a Mosquito.

Donald Gomme, whose G-Plan factory was heavily involved with Mosquito-making, has told me, 'The great advantage of building aeroplane bits in wood was that we could always saw through them when necessary. Why, we had to cut the tail in half once. Easy.'

Handling wood in wartime may have been easy but obtaining the types required presented a problem. The Mosquito devoured a forest of the finest balsa wood in Ecuador. When the first strips of this wood arrived on his desk Rex King, at that time the Assistant Experimental Manager, stuck his thumb in it. He exploded: 'What? This pappy wood? Don't be damned silly. It's not strong enough.' But nearly eight thousand Mosquitos were built in Britain, Canada and Australia from 'this pappy

Freeman (left) at a meeting of the Air Council.

wood', sandwiched between layers of birch.

The Mosquito contributed to a shortage not only of balsa but also of best-quality Canadian yellow birch and Sitka spruce. During the war Douglas fir had to be substituted for these two woods as supplies ran down. English ash is rarer than ever today as a result of this wartime demand. 'It will take fifty years to replace the best timber cut down during the war,' Donald Gomme reflected sadly as we talked in his G-Plan Gallery at Hanover Square.

Improvisation, according to timber available, dictated adjustments in the adhesives being used. Here, Gomme told me, the furniture industry, with its special knowledge of synthetic resins, was of considerable value to the aircraft builders. Glue problems beset the Mosquito from its earliest moments at Salisbury Hall. The first Mosquito sent to India came literally 'unstuck'.

The men working on the prototype were confronted with the same difficulty that has puzzled almost every schoolboy model builder in his time. The glue, made from powder and water, was apt to set too fast. Later the synthetic resins suggested by Donald Gomme helped to keep Mosquitos together as solidly as the hardy furniture his factory was also producing for the barrack blocks of Britain.

Meanwhile at the manor house the first Mosquito was nearing completion. Throughout the summer of 1940 the 'cottage industry' had developed until nearly a hundred men and women were passing through the sandbagged entrance and crossing the moat to work every day. In spite of the increase of numbers of those in the know, careful security measures were observed. Even the local doctor, arriving to

16

Freeman and his 'Folly'. Left to right: Hon. R. G. Casey; Major Hereward de Havilland; Mr A. S. Butler and Sir Wilfrid Freeman.

examine a case of suspected appendicitis, was led blindfold to his patient.

In the house, Bishop and his team worked long hours like dedicated people, only stopping to recharge themselves with cups of tea taken in the sunshine on the lawn. Somewhat incongruously, the milk for the tea came straight from the cow shed alongside the 'shop' where the Mosquito was being built.

On 3rd November 1940, the first Mosquito left Salisbury Hall for Hatfield, in disguise. As the 60-foot 'Queen Mary' trailer, all humps and lumps, turned out of the gravel drive into the main London to Birmingham road, it might have been freighting the Loch Ness Monster.

By coincidence, 3rd November was also the day on which Wilfrid Freeman officially left Lord Beaverbrook after his first spell at the Ministry of Aircraft Production. On this day it was announced that Lord Beaverbrook had 'consented to release' Freeman to assist the new Chief of the Air Staff, Sir Charles Portal.

Freeman was not enthusiastic about serving as Vice Chief of the Air Staff. In his heart of hearts he believed he could best serve the interests of the Air Force and the nation as Air Member for Development and Production attached to the civilian Ministry. It was, however, entirely characteristic of Wilfrid Freeman's modesty and sense of service that he should have remarked at the time, 'It is not for me to judge where I can most usefully serve.'

But the fact remains that he did not put down his production portfolio until the day the first Mosquito left Salisbury Hall, and 'Freeman's Folly', ordered off the drawing-board, became an aeroplane.

Chapter 4
Then There Were Two

'A maiden flight is more of an ordeal for those left behind on the ground than for the man in the aeroplane.' John E. Walker, the de Havilland Chief Engine Installation Engineer, was speaking eighteen years after sharing the adventure of the first Mosquito's maiden flight with Geoffrey de Havilland.

In 1940 this sandy-headed young man was an assistant designer in charge of engine installation and a member of Bishop's 'first eleven' at Salisbury Hall. On 25th of November he was at work in the Salisbury Hall ballroom when a colleague yelled through the door, 'For heaven's sake come quickly! Something terrible has happened.'

Salisbury Hall was on tenterhooks about the new aeroplane. Bishop's men knew that the Mosquito must surely be almost ready to fly. For a second the draughtsmen sat paralysed with horror at their drawing-boards. Then they ran out after their colleague into the garden behind the house. In a moment they saw that the catastrophe was not serious. The rotting and rickety wooden plank bridge which spanned the moat had split, tumbling Peters of the design team into the green and icy water. The laughter of the rescuers rang out across the meadows, the high-pitched double laughter of mirth and relief.

John Walker was helping to fish Peters out when the girl at the switchboard in the kitchen called him to the telephone. Geoffrey de Havilland was on the line, the test-pilot son of 'D.H.'.

'Come over to Hatfield,' he said. 'The boiler is ready.'

Twenty-three days earlier at Hatfield the dismembered Mosquito had been lifted limb by limb from the 'Queen Mary' trailer and carried into the old Tiger Moth paint shop. A 'come down' after Salisbury Hall, this was the only space that could be spared in 1940 for an untried aeroplane. Priority was still for Oxford production and Hurricane repair.

Very soon the buzz got round. Something exciting and different was happening in the old paint shop; a rather special job. Men walking to the more workaday production lines noticed that the roof of the shop had been reinforced by corrugated iron. A blast wall of eighteen-inch brick was being built and those working inside knew that a wooden prop had been put up to help keep a roof over the head of the first Mosquito.

Ramshackle yet cosy, this shelter with its flimsy fortification against enemy high explosive was sentimentally named 'The Mosquito Home' by the men who now began the frustrating task of piecing the prototype together. Rex King recalls, 'Things didn't seem to fit as well as they had down at Salisbury Hall.' Like Humpty Dumpty, the new aeroplane with its fuselage designed in two 'Easter egg' sections just wouldn't be put together again.

Delay in reassembly bred a new anxiety, fear that Jerry would destroy the prototype on the ground. Recently, the de Havilland Hatfield headquarters had experienced its worst blow of the war when a Ju88, sweeping low over the airfield, bounced four bombs off the turf into the sheet metal shop and the Technical School. Twenty-one workers were killed and seventy wounded in an accurate low-level pinpoint attack of

The camouflaged prototype outside the 'Mosquito Home' — the old Tiger Moth paint shop at Hatfield. *(British Aerospace)*

The prototype, W4050, at Salisbury Hall in 1972. *(Stuart Howe)*

the type of which the Mosquito crews were three years later to become the masters. The Ju88 was shot down and the German pilot recognized as a former pupil of the de Havilland Technical School. He knew the way.

Had the enemy mounted a similar and deliberate attack on the Mosquito Home, this story might have ended here. As it was, the prototype of the first aircraft to bomb Berlin in daylight survived sixty-eight high-explosive bombs scattered around Hatfield during the autumn of 1940.

The most anxious moment came on the night of 24th-25th November as the prototype, now a proud entity and soon to have a number (W4050),[1] stood silently waiting in the Mosquito Home for her maiden flight on the morrow. At midnight Rex King drove up in his old Minx to take a last look round. He was switching off the ignition when two disturbing things happened. He heard the all too familiar drone, drone, drone of bombers overhead. And then the car caught fire. King knew that Hitler's bomb aimers were attracted to fires like moths to light. Quickly he found a CO_2 bottle and doused the flames. The bombers passed over on their way to plaster the industrial Midlands. They had missed a rare opportunity — the chance, perhaps, of the war in the air.

[1] The first number it bore was the makers serial number, E0234.

20

The next morning when Walker arrived at Hatfield the new aeroplane was being wheeled out to the edge of the grass airfield. There was no runway in those days.

The first Mosquito wore bright yellow. Behind her walked her attendants, each with an armful of brown sacks, ready to drape the wings and the fuselage if a daylight raid developed. The sacking was her disguise on the ground. In the air her 'tarty' make-up would advertise her to ground gunners and fighter pilots as a prototype aircraft. 'Freeman's Folly' was far too secret for her graceful silhouette and special features to be circulated.

The two men who were to take her up contrasted drably with their machine. Geoffrey de Havilland and John Walker wore dark-blue flying overalls. The dazzling whites so familiar in peacetime civilian flying had disappeared with the declaration of war.

Pilot and engineer climbed into the cockpit, de Havilland to the pilot's seat on the port side, Walker beside him. Both men wiggled their parachute packs into the bare steel cavities which were custom-built for airmen's podgy backsides. The pilot squared himself off to the control column and instrument panel and discovered, as every other Mosquito pilot later discovered, that the seat was set at a very slight angle. A disconcerting necessity of design in the compact cockpit.

The engineer bent forward to close the tiny hatch through which he had climbed, and fastened his safety belt. As he did so he reckoned that it would be the devil of an aeroplane to leave in a hurry. He was the first of the hundreds of navigators who were to be sobered by this chilling reflection.

Walker looked towards de Havilland, who had started his cockpit check, and felt reassured. The Mosquito's future — his personal destiny — both were in one of the best pair of flying hands in British civil aviation. Moreover, should anything go wrong, Geoffrey de Havilland knew when to bale out. Before the war he had jumped from an experimental machine, after first ordering his companion to leave. The companion was a young test pilot, who had graduated from a de Havilland apprenticeship — John Cunningham.

The men with the less enviable role of waiting on the ground watched the yellow aeroplane taxi to the take-off position. The de Havilland hierarchy were there: Walker, who had visited the Air Ministry with Captain de Havilland in 1938 to suggest the fast unarmed bomber; Bishop, the apprentice who had worked his way up to the post of Chief Designer; Clarkson, the aerodynamicist who with Bishop had visited Rumball & Edwards and helped to secure Salisbury Hall.

In their centre, head and shoulders above his colleagues except for the lean figure of Assistant Chief Designer Tim Wilkins, stood a tall, stooping man in an old raincoat and soft hat — 'D.H.', the airman and dreamer who thirty years earlier had flown his first aeroplane while a

W4050, the prototype, is tested. Geoffrey de Havilland races her across the grass airfield before take-off. *(British Aerospace)*

young engineer named Frank Hearle lay flat on the ground to report whether there was so much as an inch of daylight between the wheels and the grass.

And this day his elder son Geoffrey, who had been born in 1910 at Crux Easton, Hampshire, near the site and during the period of his father's first flying experiments, was to fly the DH98.

On the far side of the airfield the Mosquito was moving forward. Faster and faster she sped across the grass, slap into the wind, tail up. But she did not leave the ground, and Geoffrey brought her back to the take-off position. There was nothing amiss. The test pilot had raced her across the aerodrome with both Merlin engines at full power to sample his fore and aft control. He was satisfied. Again the Mosquito began to move forward. In seconds she was in the air.

De Havilland climbed her to 15,000 feet. Everything was normal. He flew for forty-five minutes checking aileron and engine control and returned to make a perfect landing and to taxi towards his father.

Test pilot and engineer dropped out of the belly hatch, the first of the many Mosquito crews who were to bless the wooden aeroplane for a safe return. Geoffrey reported enthusiastically to his father and to Alan S.

Sir Geoffrey de Havilland's test pilot son, Geoffrey. He died when the DH108 experimental jet aircraft broke up in the air on 27th September 1946.

Butler, Chairman of the company. This was as rewarding a moment for Butler the business man, as it was for father and son.[1]

Long before the second Salisbury Hall Mosquito was ready to fly it became obvious outside Hatfield that Bishop and his team had produced a winner. At the airfield Geoffrey de Havilland treated official visitors to some remarkable demonstrations of the Mosquito's manoeuvrability.

On 20th April 1941, Lord Beaverbrook, the Minister of Aircraft Production, showed off the new aeroplane to General Arnold of the United States. De Havilland was inspired that day. He screamed the Mosquito across the airfield at 400 m.p.h. in level flight and followed with a series of upward rolls. Arnold could scarcely believe his eyes. The pilot was manoeuvring with one propeller feathered. Six days later the American air chief left for Washington. There was a new bulge in his despatch case — the Mosquito drawings.

The British test pilot's demonstrations of the Mosquito had appeared all the more devastating in its context, for it followed a fly-past of American lend-lease aircraft, all of which were pedestrian in comparison.

The prototype was now numbered W.4050, and Geoffrey de Havilland flew the aircraft to Boscombe Down for its RAF acceptance trials. There was a sickening moment when he arrived at the RAF station. He heard a loud cracking noise and discovered that a piece of wood had given in the fuselage.

Boscombe telephoned Hatfield, where Bishop kept a Hornet Moth standing by for just such an emergency. The chief designer collected his colleague Fred Plumb, the Experimental Manager, and flew to the maimed Mosquito, the only Mosquito in existence.

At Boscombe Bishop and Plumb applied first aid. Like a surgeon who draws patterns on a patient's stomach, Bishop chalked the side of the fuselage. Then Plumb went to work. He patched the crack with plywood and put a spruce member across the break. The patched-up prototype continued its career and passed the acceptance trials with flying colours.

With only one precious Mosquito in the air and the ever-present danger that some disaster might befall her, there was an urgent need to complete the second Salisbury Hall machine. If precedent were followed, there would now be a frustrating repetition of putting Humpty together again in the Mosquito Home, and several weeks of wasted effort.

One evening in the 'local' Fred Plumb drained his glass and jokingly said to Geoffrey:

'Why don't you fly her out of the field at the back?'

Geoffrey's eyes twinkled and Plumb, who had merely thrown out a pub idea, realized to his horror that he had started something. He pictured the meadow sloping gently upwards from the moat, the hedge

---

[1] In December 1921, when de Havilland were experiencing a very sticky time financially, Mr Butler, a young flying enthusiast, called to order a £3,000 private aeroplane. That month he bought 7,500 shares for £7,500. He was elected chairman in 1924, and retired in 1950.

Sir Wilfrid Freeman, in characteristic attitude, talks to US General Arnold who had shown great interest in the Mosquito from the earliest days.

across the middle and the two ancient trees. It couldn't really be done.

Next morning the Salisbury Hallites were astonished to see a familiar figure striding backwards and forwards across the field. Geoffrey de Havilland was already pacing out his minimum runway for take-off across this very rough ground. 'That hedge will have to go; so will one of the trees,' he muttered. But the pilot had not reckoned on the feelings of Farmer Dixon in the matter. The farmer of this land, a dour Scot, was at the flyer's side.

'It's impossible,' he said. 'You canna do it. First, because I want to sow. Second, you canna muck about with the hedges and trees. And that's final.'

Farmer and airman looked hard at one another. Each had his own sense of war responsibility.

'It will save a lot of time if I can fly the boiler out of here,' de Havilland said, looking at the hedge.

Farmer Dixon pleaded, 'But that hedge is a fine old hawthorn. Dig it up and it will never grow again. Besides, it's been there a very long time.'

A compromise was reached. The trees would remain but the farmer

The men who watched the first flight, with the man who flew her — see key below.

1. R. W. Fitch (Air Ministry)
2. John Walker
3. C. T. Wilkins
4. Fred Plumb
5. R. E. Bishop
6. Sir Geoffrey de Havilland
7. Geoffrey de Havilland
8. R. M. Clarkson
9. M. Herrod Hempsall
10. George Gibbins

agreed to lose a section of the hedge, enough to allow the Mosquito through at take-off.

'But mind you get your boiler ready in time. I've got my field to sow.' In the early hours of 13th May 1941, S.S. Obersturmführer Karl Richard Richter, former adjutant to the notorious Sudetenland Gauleiter, Henlein, landed by parachute in a field close to Salisbury Hall.

In hiding, Richter occupied himself by burying his parachute, flying suit, pistol, food and radio transmitter. He remained in the wood until darkness fell on 14th May. Then, smoothing down the last handfuls of mossy soil over the tell-tale swastika stamped on his flying helmet, the German officer assumed correctly that his descent had been undetected. He frisked himself down, consulted a map and a pocket compass and walked out on to the main road. The S.S. man resembled the complete Hollywood spy. Debonair in a camel-hair coat and trilby hat, he strolled towards the roundabout at London Colney.

Poor Richter! His career at large in England lasted a mere twenty minutes. It was misfortune that a lorry driver should pull up and ask him the way. Being arrogant by nature, Richter was rude. Furthermore, he indulged his testiness in a foreign accent. English lorry drivers do not expect guttural impoliteness from country gents in camel-hair coats late at night. This driver continued to the roundabout and reported his encounter to War Reserve Police Constable A. J. Scott.

When investigated, Richter produced an identity card which announced him as an alien with an address in London. This was the German's second mistake. The time was now 11.45 p.m. Constable Scott knew that aliens were subject to an 11 p.m. curfew. Richter was executed at Wandsworth Prison on 10th December 1941. It may, of course, have been a coincidence that he landed near Salisbury Hall; but, on the other hand . . .

The day after the spy's arrest a tractor trundled the second Mosquito to the top of the meadow behind Salisbury Hall. Bright in her new yellow paint, the fighter prototype bumped stiffly across the furrows like a seized-up athlete just out of a mustard bath. In the ballroom, draughtsmen downed set squares and came out to cheer. Ground crew backed her tail into the hedge at the far end of the field. In the cockpit Geoffrey de Havilland gave the 'thumbs up' to his passenger. It was Fred Plumb, paying for the idea he had had in the pub.

The take-off was dicey but uneventful, excepting for the loss of the canopy as the Mosquito banked round the tower of Shenley Mental Hospital and set course for Hatfield. The prototype's abnormally heavy wheels — they were Flamingo spares — helped her over the uneven ground. It was like putting a sprint champion into gumboots, but the airliner's wheels safely sped the light wooden machine off the heavy agricultural land and out of the farmer's hair. For the remainder of the war, Farmer Dixon was left in peace to Dig for Victory.

Chapter 5
Operational

In Whitehall, Sir Wilfrid Freeman, new Vice Chief of the Air Staff, learned that at last there were two yellow Mosquitos in the sky — the reconnaissance-bomber and fighter prototypes. At this period Freeman wished to find a replacement for the nippy D.-type Spitfires employed on long-range photographic reconnaissance. Five days before Geoffrey de Havilland flew the Mosquito from the meadow, the one remaining D.-type Spitfire in photo-reconnaissance service at that time was lost over Stettin. This was a misfortune that at once magnified the need for the new, if untried, Mosquito in this role.

The split construction of the Mosquito fuselage greatly facilitated the fitting of the internal equipment, after which the two halves were bonded together. *(British Aerospace)*

A bomber Mosquito in the making. Here, the inner fuselage skin and the between-skin structural members are being fitted, while steel bands are being used behind to give the required pressure for bonding the skins together on a completed fuselage half.
(*British Aerospace*)

But first Freeman and the Air Force faced a new threat. The Admiralty made a major bid for a large quota from forthcoming Mosquito production. There was a history to this demand. When Freeman had pushed through the order for fifty B1/40's, the Admirals, perhaps inherently less inhibited about building in wood, had shown more enthusiasm for the conception of the new aeroplane than the Air Marshals. Now, the Admiralty was obdurately pressing the Ministry of Aircraft Production for Mosquitos — as speed target towers!

This demand persisted until Lord Beaverbrook, armed with ammunition supplied by Freeman, deflected it on a point of common sense; the waste of two Merlin engines for target towing, a waste which Freeman, in his blunt manner, termed a 'lunacy'.

The Vice Chief of the Air Staff was eager now to put his 'Folly' to the only true test for any untried military aircraft — operational service. And indeed, under his spur, the Mosquito was soon to make a far more rewarding contribution to the Navy's war than ever it could have managed as a target tower.[1] This was upon its introduction to active service with No. 1 Photographic Reconnaissance Unit of the RAF's Coastal Command.

[1] In the course of time the Mosquito did descend to the humble duty of target towing. Some sixteen Mosquitos flown by civilians under contract, among them a woman pilot, Mrs Veronica Volkerz, were still towing targets round Britain in 1958.

This view of a 'bombing-up' gives a graphic idea of the fire-power concentrated in a Mosquito's nose — four 20 mm cannon and four machine guns.

Squadron Leader Rupert Clerke of No. 1 Photographic Reconnaissance Unit flew the first Mosquito operational sortie on 18th September 1941. Clerke was 25, and a rare bird in the RAF. Stepson of Air Chief Marshal Sir Edgar Ludlow-Hewitt, he had joined the peacetime service from Eton. His companion on this sortie was Sergeant Sowerbutts, a 32-year-old Margate hairdresser who had volunteered for the Air Force and was now a navigator/radio-operator. Clerke and Sowerbutts set off at 11.30 a.m. They were bound for the borders of France and Spain, where intelligence was reporting German troop movements along the frontier; activity that indicated Hitler's imminent occupation of Franco's neutral, but Axis-leaning, Spain. Their Mosquito, W.4055, was unarmed and defenceless but for its speed, Clerke's guile, the skinned eyes of Sowerbutts, and radio silence.

Squadron Leader Clerke had come to this crack Coastal Command unit from No. 79 Squadron, a Battle of Britain Hurricane squadron. He missed his gun button, but he had learned to survive on his wits flying an unarmed reconnaissance Spitfire on lone long-ranging sorties over Scandinavia.

This September day Clerke was not alone. There was a companion with whom to share the anxiety of searching the blue above for hostile fighters. On practice flights the Squadron Leader had quickly appreciated the Mosquito for its handling qualities. But he had yet to learn to co-exist in the cockpit. The Hurricane and the Spitfire had developed a breed of supremely independent operators.

Squadron Leader Clerke climbed the Mosquito to an altitude below trail level and applied one of the golden rules of photo-recce. He told Sowerbutts to keep a sharp lookout for tell-tale fighter trails. He also warned him that he would slap his hand any time he caught it wandering dangerously close to the morse key. Sowerbutts was signals trained.

High over the Bay of Biscay, Clerke set course towards the Spanish sunshine and estimated that he ought to reach the Franco-Spanish border at siesta time.

It would be gratifying to launch the story of the Mosquito's operational career by recording a brilliant success. Historically this cannot be. 'Freeman's Folly' failed the Old Etonian and the hairdresser that day. Over the Bay W.4055's generator packed up and the batteries ran down. Squadron Leader Clerke and Sergeant Sowerbutts, obliged to abandon the sortie, returned to base empty-handed.

On the way home in the afternoon, the technical trouble extended to an alarmingly haywire air speed indicator. A bee, brave but distrait, had got jammed in the tiny static vent of the indicator's pitot tube. Less technically, by gumming up the works, the silly bee had helped to take the sting out of the first Mosquito mission.

Two days afterwards, Flight Lieutenant Alistair Taylor flew the Mosquito's first successful sortie, a reconnaissance of the Bordeaux coastline. Next day he photographed Heligoland and Sylt. The aircraft was W.4055. Ten weeks later Taylor, now a Squadron Leader and the first RAF officer to be awarded three DFC's, failed to return from a recce over Trondheim and Bergen. It was the first Mosquito loss.

Hit by flak over Norway, Taylor courageously headed out to crash at sea and save the Mosquito from enemy investigation. Taylor and his companion, Sergeant Horsfall, perished with W.4055.

A new aeroplane, like a new boy at school, is traditionally suspect. Service pilots love their old faithfuls and tend to cling to them. They are the friends they really know. Blessed and cursed alternatively for their attributes and shortcomings, they remain adored until the new aircraft has earned its own respect. 'Freeman's Folly' — the Mossie — was to become beloved, and to establish a legend, sooner than most. At No. 1 PRU, Squadron Leader Clerke, expedited the process, initiating new Mosquito pilots with a really murderous ride.

But in the beginning the photo-recce pilots, accustomed to sallying forth high, fast and dandily in their candy-pink Spitfires, were a trifle doubtful when Geoffrey de Havilland flew their first wooden two-seater into Benson. Moreover, the historically-informed were able to heighten the normal ration of suspicion with a singular fact. This DH98 was the first de Havilland designed and built aircraft to be flown regularly in RAF Operational Squadron service since the 125 m.p.h. DH9A in 1917.

No. 1 PRU's first Mosquito had arrived two months before Squadron Leader Clerke's maiden sortie. In August two more Mosquitos were delivered. By the end of October five additional new aircraft had arrived. Now the politicians had to see and touch for themselves the wooden aeroplane which was saving scarce metal and skilled workers. Some days the pilots feared the Mosquito might turn them into an air circus. There were joy rides for VIP's. Squadron Leader Clerke flew Mr Attlee, the Lord Privy Seal, and Sir Archibald Sinclair, the Air Minister. There were rides, too, for Russians. A Soviet Colonel, inspired by the experience, drove off to Hatfield and made urgent representations to de Havilland's for a Mosquito factory in the Soviet Union.

On another occasion No. 1 PRU's C.O., Wing Commander Geoffrey Tuttle, fought a mock dog-fight in a Spitfire against Clerke in a Mosquito. It was a command performance for the King and Queen.

The Mosquito very soon sold itself to the pilots. They forgave its sins in grateful acceptance of its virtues. The tail shimmy, the swing on take-off, a leaking cockpit, smouldering engine cowlings, and a host of teething troubles were more than counter-balanced by the credit side. Here was a great little aeroplane. It would bring you home on one engine. It could produce the speed to close and engage tip-and-run enemy night bombers. It offered the range, not only for bloodless photographic reconnaissance but also for destructive intrusion over enemy airfields. And one of these fine days it would undoubtedly bomb Berlin in daylight.

Major Hereward de Havilland, who was always dropping in at Mosquito stations in a flying club Moth, reported to 'D.H.', his elder brother, 'The machine is being accepted by aircrew as something quite outstanding.' After an early visit to No. 1 PRU he wrote: 'In my experience it is the only aircraft which has initially not been branded by pilots as a death trap in one way or another. On the other hand the engineering and maintenance personnel, particularly the younger generation, were very much biased against it, mainly on account of the wooden construction.'

The German aircraft industry evidently had the same attitude. In September 1942 Hermann Goering, addressing the heads of the industry, praised the Mosquito and said, 'I wish someone had brought out a wooden aircraft for me.' Our own experts had been dubious in 1938, but fortunately we had a de Havilland and a Freeman.

Goering's admiration of the wooden aeroplane was not readily shared by the maintenance men on the ground in Britain. The Mosquito had to earn their respect the hard way, selling itself to the engineers on its unexpected sturdiness. One aircraft even managed to collide with a steam roller — and lived to fight another day.

Gradually the grumbles of the maintenance staff became more good-humoured until one bright spark made a crack which went round the Air Force. All that was the matter with the Mossie, the story went, was the fact that it had two engines. A terrible waste of taxpayer's money!

Major de Havilland reported a little later: 'The Mosquito in a few months has achieved a popularity which I should think must be almost

This photo must have been taken in the United States as the Mosquito carries a USAAF serial, whereas aircraft based in the UK wore their British serial numbers with the US national insignia. *(via Stuart Howe)*

unique in that its praises are sung, not only by pilots, but also by maintenance staffs . . . Even engineer officers have been known to walk up and pat its fuselage.'

In the meantime Major de Havilland nourished the public relations work the aircraft was doing for itself by inviting parties of pilots over to Hatfield for squash matches. More serious matters, such as ideas for modifications, were discussed afterwards in the local.

The first Mosquito bomber, night fighter and intruder operations began within weeks of each other. Spring, which had been propitious for the new aeroplane at Salisbury Hall in 1940 and 1941, smiled upon her fortunes again in 1942. In April the aircraft's prospects blossomed beyond the click-and-run camera missions of No. 1 Photographic Reconnaissance Unit and advanced towards the first of the many further 'editions' forecast by Freeman. No. 105 Squadron, the first Mosquito bomber squadron, prepared for action with nine aircraft. No. 157, first Mosquito night fighter squadron, took delivery of 19 aircraft. No. 151, a Defiant squadron, was re-equipped with 19 Mosquitos.

But the winter months had been frustrating for the aircrew awaiting the Mosquitos. No. 105 were particularly browned off, the morale barometer dropping from a high point in the previous November when Geoffrey de Havilland had personally flown in their first machine, to zero as the operationless months passed. On 15th November, enthralled by the arrival of their first Mosquito, No. 105 officially recorded: 'Another great day in the history of 105 Squadron; even the Spitfire pilots of 152 Squadron were impressed'.

Pilots, bored with bumbling about in Blenheims, showed off the new bomber to the Spitfire boys — the bomber which was as fast as a fighter. Since November, however, slow delivery of the remainder of the new aircraft had reduced the pulse rate of the squadron. Mundane matters became momentous, so that it was a highlight when Squadron Leader Channer collected a Magister which had been forced-landed in a field by two escaping German prisoners-of-war. This event, and the staging by the station dramatic society of *The Case of the Frightened Lady*, found its way into the Operation Record Book. There was little else to report.

Through February, March and April, No. 105 waited and groaned. For they realized that as each month went by the unarmed Mosquito would become less of a match for the improving performance of enemy fighters.

Production was slow. At Hatfield, de Havilland, bedevilled by official changes of mind over the number of each type on order, was seriously hindered by all the chopping and changing. Freeman's successors at the Ministry of Aircraft Production, having long since departed from the first clear-cut specification of the B1/40 as an unarmed speed bomber, were permutating photo-recce, bomber, fighter, and trainer Mosquitos out of the joint order for 50 bombers with the zeal of a pools syndicate, but without much luck. They even asked for two turret fighters at one stage

— an abortion that almost ruined the Mosquito's prospects for ever.

At the end of April, the Luftwaffe made a sharp attack on Norwich. To complete their exasperation, members of 105 Squadron found themselves in the galling situation of digging for casualties in the rubble with police and ARP workers. But very soon it was to be their turn to attack.

As a night fighter the Mosquito was not much quicker off the mark. Here again there was a maddening time-lag. No. 157 Squadron was formed on 13th December 1941, pilotless and without aircraft. Over a month later, No. 157's first C.O., Wing Commander Gordon Slade, who had flown the prototype at Boscombe Down during the acceptance trials, landed a dual-control Mosquito at Castle Camps airfield near Saffron Walden. Awaiting the C.O.'s arrival was one of his flight commanders — Squadron Leader Rupert Clerke. It was a dispiriting situation for two of the very few pilots with any Mosquito experience and eager to blood the new aircraft as a night fighter. Here they were, one trainer between them, and stationed on a hangarless airfield without proper shelter against wind and rain for the Mosquito's plywood body.

In early March No. 157's aircraft were still absent. The ground staff, who were digging for victory round the squadron offices, had reached the tennis court when at the end of the month Wing Commander Slade's Mosquitos arrived. By mid-May, night patrols and day tennis were in full swing at Castle Camps.

At Wittering, No. 151 became the second night-fighter Mosquito squadron. But trade was slack and by the end of May each squadron had yet to notch up a certainty.

During the night of 30th May, the Station commander at Wittering, already obsessed with his new Mosquito, was patrolling. He obtained 40 contacts on his interception radar set in addition to eight visuals, but he did not once open fire. It was the night of the thousand-bomber raid on Cologne. Group Captain Basil Embry[1] was practising on the outgoing traffic.

[1] Air Chief Marshal Sir Basil Embry, GCB, DSO (3 bars), DFC, AFC. In a wartime letter to Sir John Slessor he called the Mosquito 'the finest aeroplane, without exception, that has ever been built in this country.'

The production line at Hatfield. The Mosquitos are FB.VIs. Note the fuselage shells in the centre. *(via Stuart Howe)*

A wintry scene showing an NF.XIX of 157 Squadron. The serial is partly obscured but could be MM654. *(via Stuart Howe)*

In the small hours of 31st May, as the four-engine heavies were droning home and Embry was turning in, Squadron Leader A. R. Oakeshott was awakened. At 4 a.m. Oakeshott was airborne on the first Mosquito bomber mission of the war. His brief: to bomb Cologne in daylight, to stoke up the fires of the night before, and to keep the sirens wailing.

Five times that day No. 105's singleton unarmed Mosquitos ranged over the column of smoke which towered to 14,000 feet over the German city. Each Mosquito carried one 500-lb. bomb and two 250-lb. bombs. Each sortie could be little more than a buzz-in-and-sting affair after the plastering Cologne had received from the heavy bombers overnight. In destructive power these single Mosquitos were playing only a minor and supporting role. But in terms of morale it was a star part.

The waif-like aeroplane which 'D.H.' had decided to 'do anyway' during the Munich crisis, kept Hitler's sirens busy all day after Cologne's terrible night. From Bishop's drawing-board in the peaceful, moated manor house, the Mosquito had already come a long way and this was only the beginning of the story.

In the late afternoon of 31st May, Squadron Leader Channer flew No. 105's last sortie of the day. Approaching Cologne at roof level, he climbed to 1,000 feet and shallow-dived at 380 m.p.h. over the dazed city. Then, skimming homewards at a low level, Channer observed a phenomenon that struck him as being rather curious. The cattle in the fields had taken no notice of the aircraft until it was well past them. This bovine disinterest in the Mosquito did a major disservice to Hitler. For Squadron Leader Channer's barn-top experience had introduced the DH98 to its most exciting role as a low-level blaster of selected targets. Coupled with Embry's fanatical regard for the Mosquito, Channer's discovery augured ill for the enemy.

These two events at the end of May heralded the future hair-raising operations of Air Vice Marshal Embry's prison-breaking, train-busting, Gestapo-baiting No. 2 Group Mossies.

Meanwhile the wooden wonder of the metal airframe era had first to overcome new opposition at a high level. Not in the hostile skies, but on the ground in Britain.

36

Chapter 6
The Air Staff Have Doubts

Up in the gusty tiltyard over Germany, Mosquito crews in ones, twos and threes began to gather experience. Like Squadron Leader Clerke and his fellow photographic reconnaissance pilots, the bomber 'drivers' soon developed an almost animal instinct for survival when hunted in the chase.

Pilots ordered navigators to kneel up on their hard metal seats and face aft in search of enemy fighters. They learned that with good 'notice' they could keep out of range of fighters' guns provided the Germans did not possess a very large advantage in altitude. Tail-warning radar, an electronic eyes-in-the-back device, was not to be installed in Mosquitos until very much later in the war.

Back at base the pilots of the first unarmed bombers practised their powers of evasion in friendly combat with a pair of tame Spitfires. On the ground they sought constantly for ideas that would squeeze extra speed out of the aircraft. One measure, obviously not very popular with the ground crews but much favoured by pilots and navigators, was the maintenance of such a high polish that each Mosquito would have put the toecaps of a Buckingham Palace sentry to shame. This was no 'bull'. A high polish could increase a Mosquito's speed by as much as 8 m.p.h. Only the speed of a cruising schoolboy out on a bicycle ride, but a mortal margin when service aircraft and skilled lives were at stake.

There were now two Mosquito squadrons in Bomber Command, No. 105 and No. 139 (Jamaica) Squadron. No. 139 was in the usual position of new Mosquito units. It possessed no aircraft. But this dismal situation did not deter the freshly posted aircrew from facing the enemy.

On 2nd July 1942, No. 139's Commanding Officer, Wing Commander Oakeshott, borrowed a Mossie from No. 105, his old squadron, and led a daylight low-level attack on the heavily defended submarine slipways at Flensburg. Group Captain MacDonald, Station Commander at Horsham

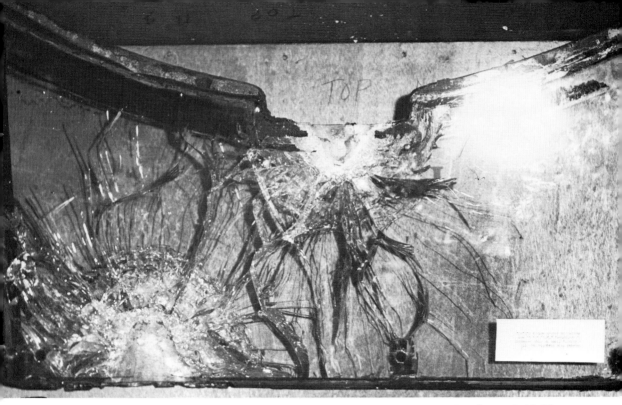

Bullet-proof windscreen of a night fighter Mosquito, shattered by bullets from a Ju88. The pilot, John Cunningham, escaped with splinters in his face.

St Faith, where the two squadrons were then based, flew another of No. 105's machines.

The raid was not a success. Two aircraft out of the formation of five were lost and each pilot who managed to survive flak and fighters only did so after a frightening and hazardous experience. Among them, Squadron Leader Houlston was chased by three Fw 190's and Flight Lieutenant Hughes, after being hit by flak, was chased for twenty minutes by three Me109's.

The reputation of the Mosquito, already ailing at Bomber Command (where it had never been popular), sank even lower when the identities of the two missing pilots were learned. Group Captain MacDonald became a prisoner-of-war and Wing Commander Oakeshott was last seen over the North Sea on the homeward journey. There was a fighter on his tail. In one Mosquito raid Horsham St Faith had lost the Station Commander and No. 139 Squadron's Commanding Officer.

Nine days later, on a summer's night, six Mosquitos, flying in two formations of three, made a new attempt on the U-boat slipways at Flensburg — an attack that was carried out partly as a diversion for a Lancaster visit to Danzig.

Squadron Leader Channer, who had followed Oakeshott over Cologne, led the first formation. All three aircraft bombed successfully with incendiary and high explosive.

The story was sadly different with the second formation, for none of the aircraft even reached the target. One turned back after losing his companion pilots in low clowd. The other two, Sergeant Rowland and Flight Lieutenant Hughes, flew on towards Flensburg until Rowland was suddenly obliged to part company with Hughes. Both pilots were racing across the rooftops, heading straight for the U-boats, when Rowland felt a tremendous jarring sensation. He looked across at his navigator, Sergeant Carreck — and there sitting in Carreck's lap was a sizeable portion of a German chimney pot. There was also a very large hole in the side of the wooden fuselage and the port engine was beginning to vibrate badly. Sergeant Rowland realized he could no longer keep up with the Flight Lieutenant's aircraft. On the point of turning for home, Rowland took one last look at Hughes. He was *below* him. And that was the last that anybody saw of Hughes and his Mosquito.

The Mosquito did not seem to be getting away with it as a bomber. It was therefore only human that critics of the original concept of an unarmed speed bomber should begin to agitate against the operation of the aeroplane in this role.

In 1942 air policy matters were still partially influenced by the trench truths of the Kaiser's war. The young airmen of 1914-1918 were the Air Marshals of the 1940's. They had matured — the far-sighted Wilfrid Freeman among them — in the dog-fight tradition of charging the enemy head-on. Seconded from regiments, they learned to fly and to fight as army officers in that cherished aerial cavalry, the Royal Flying Corps. The suggestion of sending airmen out to bomb the enemy without arming them to fight their way home, went very much against the grain with such men as Portal, Chief of the Air Staff, Ludlow-Hewitt, Inspector General of the Royal Air Force, and Harris, C-in-C of Bomber Command.

The Embry-Bennett generation of Air Force leaders still awaited the recognition and promotion that was to enable these younger officers to employ the Mosquito bomber with devastating accuracy and effect.

The One Thousand Bomber Raid was the breath of life to the C-in-C of Bomber Command, whose single-minded battering of Germany has since marched him into history as Bomber Harris. Air Marshal Sir Arthur Harris was busy making it abundantly clear at this stage of the war that he did not want the Mosquito, either as a bomber or as a fighter-bomber, in any of his squadrons. He was building up a force of heavy bombers to blast Germany out of the war. The enemy had initiated the bombing competition. Now they were to swallow a dose of their own medicine. It was to be retribution by the ladle from the heavies, not by the teaspoon with the Mosquito.

In the autumn of 1942 Major Hereward de Havilland, making his Mosquito rounds in the Leopard Moth, quickly sensed this atmosphere. He reported to Hatfield: 'Lunched at Bomber Command with Air Commodore Harrison. Harrison is the only person I have met at Bomber

Pinpoint raid on the Gestapo HQ at Oslo taken from the leading Mosquito, this photograph shows (A) dust and debris rising from the impact of a direct hit, (B) the central cupola from which the pilots could see the Nazi flag flying, and (C) the nearby University, undamaged by the raid. *(Crown Copyright)*

Command who has any enthusiasm for the Mosquito as a bomber. The C-in-C certainly has none . . .'

In the meantime, the crews of Nos. 105 and 139 Squadrons carried on their pioneer work. The more practised they became in low-level daylight bombing, the more convinced were the pilots that the Mosquito bomber could justify its existence in this dashing role. Plastering German towns with well-armed heavies was one matter, they reckoned, but with Mosquitos were already obtaining a target accuracy which could not be matched by the heavies. This marksmanship was not restricted to conventional incendiary and high-explosive bombs. On occasions pilot and navigator of a Mosquito would fortify themselves on a long low-level sortie with a bottle of beer apiece. The empties were never returned.

On the first of August, Wing Commander H. I. ('Hughie') Edwards, who had won the V.C. in a raid on Bremen during 105's Blenheim days a year earlier, took command of this squadron. Technical troubles and enemy fighters combined to harass him, and at the end of his first Mosquito month Wing Commander Edwards was faced with a 'bill' for six aircraft lost out of 45 sorties.

He had also come very close to losing his own life. On the morning of 29th August Edwards and his navigator, Pilot Officer Thomas, made a low-level attack on the switch and transformer house of a power station at Pont à Verdin. Wing Commander Edwards had just observed his bombs bursting on target when he was set upon by fighters. Enemy bullets crippled the Mosquito, but it crash-landed safely at Lympne.

For a few weeks it certainly seemed that the Mosquito in its original concept as an unarmed speed bomber amounted to a major mistake. Then, on 25th September, a special target was selected for a daylight attack at low level by four Mosquitos from No. 105 Squadron.

It was known that Quisling, the Norwegian traitor, had arranged a Nazi rally in German-occupied Oslo that day. The purposes of the raid were to break up Quisling's party, destroy Gestapo records and kill as many Gestapo officers as possible. Quisling's meeting was being held in a building above the central Norwegian torture chamber.

Before take-off Squadron Leader D. A. G. Parry and his crews were briefed that their target was a building with a high dome.

Parry led the Mosquitos up the Skaggerak. The sky was clear and blue and offered a happy hunting-ground for enemy fighters. The unarmed bombers crossed the Oslo Fjord and headed for the Norwegian capital. In the clear sunny weather the airmen easily identified the dome of the Gestapo building. And as if to pinpoint the target for them, the menacing symbol of the swastika flag fluttered before their eyes.

As Parry and his crews made straight for it, Quisling and his bodyguard pushed their way through the audience and hurried down to the cellars.

By this time a flight of Fw 190's was up. One of the Mosquitos fell victim to a Focke-Wulf, and crashed like a winged bird into a shallow lake outside the city. Later that day, while Norwegian patriots sang national songs in the streets of Oslo, the Germans fished frantically, for they had not yet learned all the secrets of the Mosquito.

In the weeks that followed, the bomber's reputation sank lower and lower, although in Germany Hermann Goering was haranguing the heads of his aircraft industry for not producing a 'Mosquito'. The Herr Reichsmarshal, anxious over the appearance of the little aeroplane and preoccupied by his belief in what it might do once production improved, had forgotten his long-standing ban on wooden construction for front-line aircraft.

On 19th September, seven days after Goering had delivered a particularly angry speech on the subject of the Mosquito to his design experts, six Mosquitos set off to surprise Berliners in the afternoon. Only one aircraft bombed the target area. The remainder were forced to break up, bomb Hamburg or jettison their bombs. One failed to return.

In Whitehall, where Goering's anxiety was not known, any belief that remained in the bomber was fast fading. But among the aircrew, as operational experience increased, so did their confidence in the aeroplane. And experience was leading to necessary modifications, the need for which could only be appreciated as a result of active service.

In these still early days for the Mosquito, some very odd things would happen. For example, on their way home from a low-level attack in daylight on a Dutch target, the crews of three Mosquitos suddenly observed their fourth member perform the most astonishing manoeuvre at ground level. The aeroplane seemed to stop, stand up on its tail and beg like a dog, then resume level flight against all the known laws.

In the tiny cockpit a frantic struggle for survival was taking place as the other Mosquito crews watched in horror. Flying Officer A. N. Bristow and Flying Officer B. W. Marshall of No. 105 Squadron were skimming home on top of the world. They had been 'in the wars' often enough lately. But this time, miracle of miracles, they had brought their beloved Mossie away from flak and fighters unscathed. There were no flak holes in the fuselage as on the Ijmuiden steel works job, from which they had only just managed to stagger home across the sea. No crash-landing lay ahead, as had been the case after the flakking received on a tea-time trip to the Flensburg U-Boats. Today it was a piece of cake.

And then it happened. Bristow suddenly fell forward over the control column, as cold as a boxer knocked out by Joe Louis. Marshall, the navigator, reacted quickly. He seized the stick and just prevented the machine from hitting the ground by yanking it savagely back. This was the moment when to the other crews the Mosquito seemed to stand on its tail, and behave more like a cartoon character than a de Havilland aircraft. Then it dawned on Marshall that he alone was conscious in an aeroplane that he hadn't the slightest idea how to fly. He pushed the stick forward, hoping that this at least would bring the Mossie off her tail. It did — and for an instant both engines cut.

At this moment Bristow came round. Blinded by blood running into both eyes, he could see nothing. Marshall's eyesight was clear but the windscreens were shattered and he could see nothing outside the cockpit. Hastily, Marshall dropped down to his bomb-aiming window in the nose. Like a guide dog leading a blind man home from a day's work, the navigator coaxed Bristow back to base, telling him, with backward kicks on his shins, how to steer. One kick for starboard, two kicks for port. At base it was dark, but Marshall gave a running commentary on the instrument readings and talked Bristow and their Mosquito down. On the fourth attempt, they made a perfect landing.

What had happened? The Mosquito had run into a flock of curlew. After this terrifying experience, a bird-proof windscreen was developed.

In the autumn weeks the pioneer bomber crews continued to add to their experience. They learned that the Mosquito's arch-enemy, the Fw 190, was 20 to 30 m.p.h. faster above 20,000 feet but that they could generally expect to pull away at near ground level.

In their bomb-aiming they began to attain a standard of accuracy that was well above the average of crews operating other types of aircraft — provided they bombed from 50-100 feet. They learned that all was not irretrievably lost if they came down in enemy territory. Flight Lieutenant Costello-Bowen and Warrant Officer Broom of No. 105 Squadron, after hitting a Dutch Pylon on their way to attack an aerodrome near Cologne, had escaped — thanks to Belgian patriots — to fight another day.

From an attack on a convoy at the estuary entrance to the Gironde they also learned that, approaching at wave-top height, the Mosquito could hit ships. The cost of this discovery was one aircraft; its crew, Bristow and Marshall.

At the end of October 1942, very nearly two years after the reassembly of the yellow prototype. W.4050, in 'The Mosquito Home' at Hatfield, the public were allowed into some of the secrets of the Mosquito. The *Daily Mail* hailed the aeroplane as a 'grandson of the Comet and a prodigal son of the Albatross'. 'Publication', the *Mail* said on 27th October, 'is permitted for the first time this morning of an illustration of Britain's new wonder plane. Some time ago, while even the name of the new super-fast bomber was still a closely guarded secret, a Mosquito crashed into the sea. High-speed launches and units of the Navy rushed to the area, and combed the sea for miles in order that not a single piece of wreckage should be left behind. The wood might have drifted into enemy hands . . .'

The Press praised the Mosquito's wooden construction, explaining that in some cases the wood was less vulnerable to gunfire than metal.

The Aeronautical Correspondent of *The Times* wrote, 'First details may now be given of the Mosquito reconnaissance-bomber, the most discussed British-made aircraft of recent times. It was designed and constructed by the de Havilland Aircraft Company and is unique among present-day operational types in being of wooden construction.'

Revelation of the Mosquito bomber through the propaganda channels of the Air Ministry and the Ministry of Information made a good story for the Press, but in fact at this moment the aeroplane could not have been in worse odour or 'more discussed' at Chief of Staff level.

With the motive of not 'wasting' the design and production capacity of de Havilland, the Air Marshals cogitated the ending of the Mosquito's career. De Havilland, it was considered, should be encouraged to turn their attention to something 'more useful'.

Papers on the Mosquito's fate passed round the rarefied heights of the Air Ministry. A few swift lines had started the little wooden aeroplane on Bishop's drawing-board at Salisbury Hall. Now a pencil stroke in Whitehall could put an end to 'Freeman's Folly', and the Mosquito would join the legion of lost causes.

Wilfrid Freeman was no longer Vice Chief of the Air Staff when the Mosquito's fate lay in the balance. He was out of the Air Force and working as a civilian for the first time in his life. His uniform, the top button still undone, the medal ribbons fading, remained in retirement on its plain wooden hanger. He never wore uniform again. Freeman was now a civil servant. In October Mr Churchill had entrusted to him the overall executive responsibility for aircraft production. He was now Chief Executive of the Ministry of Aircraft Production.

The parting of Portal and Freeman as CAS and VCAS had presented the Prime Minister with a tough decision to make. Together they had occupied the two top places of the Royal Air Force. Very old friends, they had lunched or dined once a week for several years past to exchange opinions and confidences. Portal was aged 49 and junior to Freeman in age by five years. Until his appointment as Chief of the Air Staff, he had also been junior in the service to Freeman throughout his career. Indeed, he had been Group Captain Freeman's pupil at the RAF Staff College. Here, then, was a partnership which the Prime Minister could not break up without the most serious consideration, and for several months in 1942 Mr Churchill resisted advice to offer Freeman the top job at the Ministry of Aircraft Production.

The chief pleader of this cause was Sir Charles Craven, Managing Director of Vickers-Armstrong, who had worked alongside Freeman at the Ministry of Aircraft Production earlier in the war.

At the end of Lord Beaverbrook's regime in the spring of 1941, Mr Patrick Hennessy of the Ford Motor Company, who had been chosen by the Beaver as his first production lieutenant, left with him. Hennessy's departure made a gap in the production executive and at the Prime

Minister's urgent request Sir Charles Craven returned as Controller General, to leave again just over a year later on the ground of ill health. Before his departure, Sir Charles put in the strongest possible recommendation to Mr Churchill for Sir Wilfrid to replace him. When the Prime Minister said 'no', Sir Charles wrote to him: 'I hope you will not mind my telling you how sorry I am that you do not feel justified in relieving Freeman from his present duties in order that he could succeed me. I feel that if I could have seen you I might have been able to persuade you that he is far the best man for the job.'

Craven reviewed the five years of work Freeman had put in as Air Member for Research and Development, and later Production, during the expansion of the aircraft industry.

'I learned his speed of decision at the time,' Sir Charles wrote, 'because I worked with him intimately when Vickers were building shadow factories. On one occasion I remember getting orders to proceed with one of the largest shadow factories within twenty-four hours of first discussion.

'When I worked with him as a member of the Air Council later at MAP, I realized the great respect in which he is held by the industry, and that he had a far greater knowledge of industrial affairs than any serving officer of any service.

'There are really very few so-called "Captains of Industry" experienced in great affairs. I know plenty of industrialists who are excellent production men but who would be quite useless in a government department.' Sir Charles ended, 'I have written to you solely in the interests of MAP and because I want to see my biggest war job the success it can be in the right hands.'

Three months after Sir Charles left the Ministry, Sir Wilfrid returned to carry on the work of leading the nation's endeavour in the vital realm of aircraft production, development and research. As Chief Executive at the Ministry of Aircraft Production he controlled all aspects of aircraft research, development and production and shared with the Permanent Secretary the control of all other activities not secretarial or financial. This was the sort of job in which he had always believed he could most usefully serve his country.[1]

[1] Marshal of the RAF Sir John Slessor, broadcasting in 1953 on the anniversary of the Battle of Britain, said: 'The delayed action of long selfless years of strain and overwork still adds names to the roll of those who died in battle. And high among those names will stand that of Wilfrid Freeman. It was to him, more than any other man, that the nation and the RAF owed the fact that the pilots of Fighter Command never ran short of those aircraft whose names — "Hurricane" and "Spitfire" — are now as much a part of British history as Nelson's *Victory* and *Royal Sovereign* . . . Britain was indeed fortunate in having, at a supreme crisis in her history, Freeman, a man of genius, who not only laid the foundation of the production programme in the Air Ministry before the change-over, but was later to steer it to its ultimate development as Chief Executive in the MAP . . . There were many decisions of vital importance during the years 1936 to 1939 for which the responsibility and the credit lay with Freeman. Hundred-octane fuel, the variable pitch propeller, the air rocket, for instance; and above all, the initiation of the four-engined bomber policy.

On 7th December, some weeks after he had become a civilian, Sir Wilfrid received a letter from the Air Ministry which caused him considerable alarm. It was from Air Marshal Sir Christopher Courtney, and warned him that the Mosquito's fate was once more in the balance. A recent Air Ministry minute for the Chief of Air Staff advocated dropping the idea of an unarmed speed bomber since it could never be as effective as the faster night bombers, and the heavily armed Fortresses by day.

By chance, as Courtney was writing to Freeman on 6th December, Wing Commander Edwards and his bomber Mosquitos were on their way to carry out a particularly successful low-level daylight attack on the Philips works at Eindhoven in Holland. It was a raid which was to help considerably to alter the official attitude to the Mosquito as a bomber.

On Christmas Eve, after details of the effects of the attack had been received by Dutch officials in London, the Dutch Minister called on Sir Archibald Sinclair to express on behalf of his Government the admiration they felt for the skill with which the attack on the Philips works had been planned and executed.

On Christmas Day 1942 the Air Minister wrote to Air Marshal Harris. He said (of the Dutch): 'Their admiration of the gallantry of the attacking crews was only equalled by their gratitude for the accuracy of their aim and for the consequent avoidance of increasing injury and suffering to the civilian population.'

The Mosquito could have earned no better tribute than the gratitude of those who had to watch the RAF bombs dropping on their country.

Chapter 7
Mosquito in Five Editions

Early in 1941, 'D.H.' had been anxious to blood the DH98 as a night fighter. After the heartbreaks over the unarmed bomber, he desired to obtain a decent start in life for the second 'edition' of the Mosquito. There was one pilot in the Air Force he knew he could rely upon to give the Mosquito a fair trial and assessment as a potential night fighter. If this airman's report was favourable, then the new edition would get a good send-off. 'D.H.' therefore personally approached Sir Charles Portal, Chief of the Air Staff, with an unusual request: he asked him to authorize a certain young pilot, then serving with No. 604 Beaufighter Squadron, to fly and assess the prototype of the Mosquito fighter. Portal agreed.

The pilot was Squadron Leader John Cunningham, the former de Havilland apprentice, who was now a night-fighter ace with a DSO and a DFC. On 2nd June 1941 John Cunningham became the first service pilot to fly the second Mosquito — W.4052 — eighteen days after Geoffrey de Havilland had flown this very same 'boiler' out of the meadow behind Salisbury Hall.

John Cunningham, who had been one of the first two RAF pilots to fly the Beaufighter operationally as a night fighter at the end of 1940,[1] was impressed. He put in a helpful report. There seemed to be only one drawback: in comparison with the 'Beau', the Mosquito's initial rate of climb was not so good. The Beaufighter, introduced operationally in October 1940 by Cunningham, had been a great advance on the Blenheim. Now Cunningham forecast that the handling qualities and the manoeuvrability of this little wooden wonder would vastly improve the chances of finding, closing and engaging enemy bombers in the darkness over Britain. Speed in a radar night fighter was essential. The Beaufighter was giving over 300 m.p.h., but Cunningham found that he could push W.4052 to nearly 400 m.p.h.

[1] The other was Wing Commander M. F. Anderson, DFC.

The speed and strength of the Mosquito made it difficult to stop. From one intruder patrol over Holland this aircraft returned with 300 feet of copper cable.

The delay in equipping Nos. 157 and 151, the first two night-fighter Mosquito squadrons, has already been described, but once their aircraft began to operate, their speed surprised friend and foe alike. The new night fighter appeared at a critical moment when the new Dornier 217s were making a 320-m.p.h. getaway after dropping their bombs.

Competition for the first kills was keen between Nos. 151 and 157 Squadrons. No. 151, a former Defiant squadron, notched up a probable in the early hours of 30th May 1942. This was a Heinkel 111 engaged by Flight Lieutenant Pennington, flying D.D.628 — a Mosquito much favoured, and usually flown, by Group Captain Basil Embry, the Wittering station commander. No. 151 scored their first certainty on the night of 24th June, when Wing Commander I. S. Smith, the C.O. (with Flight Lieutenant Shepherd), shot down a torpedo-carrying Heinkel 111 and a Do 217 within ten minutes of each other.

No. 157 bagged their first certainty on the night of 22nd August. It was a Dornier 217 near Southwold for Wing Commander R. G. Slade, the C.O., with Pilot Officer Truscott.

Although the Mosquito was an all-round improvement on exisiting night fighters, 'kills' did not come easily. Nor did the night-fighter Mosquito settle down to operational service without its share of teething troubles. As with the bomber version, night-fighter crews learned by trial and error.

It was soon discovered, for instance, that the flash from the .303 Browning guns could temporarily blind the pilot to anything outside the cockpit, even to the brightest stars. So No. 157's engineer officer, Flight Lieutenant Stoneman, a six-foot-seven giant, and Flight Sergeant Burge designed and made special flash eliminators to overcome the problem. In the haste to pit the night fighter against the enemy the .303's had never been fired in the air at night during gunnery trials at Boscombe Down.

On the credit side, pilots of the single-engine Defiant converted to the twin Mosquito with remarkable ease. The third Mosquito night-fighter squadron, No. 264, received its first aircraft on 4th May. Some pilots went solo on the new type after two hours in an Oxford. Others flew the Mosquito without any previous twin-engine experience. On 30th July, Squadron Leader Cooke bagged No. 264's first victim — another Do 217.

No. 85 Squadron, later to score many Mosquito night victories, were not so fortunate. This squadron received its first Mosquito on 29th July and crashed it the next day. But in October, when No. 410, a predominantly Canadian squadron, received its first Mossie, the pilots flew the aeroplane for 15 hours during the first two days and passed out seven pilots solo. They flew their Mossie before the handbook on the type arrived at the station.

Meanwhile 'trade' was fairly slack. Few enemy bombers were coming over during this period and those that did chance it seemed to favour nights when weather conditions were particularly dirty. At the end of September one notable engagement took place. Rupert Clerke, now a Wing Commander, ranging the Dutch coast in a No. 157 Squadron night fighter, destroyed a Ju 88 from a distance of 1,200 yards. No one was more surprised than himself.

Major de Havilland, maintaining his ceaseless liaison with Mosquito units in his Leopard Moth, did not, of course, restrict himself to the bomber boys. After a visit to Wittering on 12th July 1942 he reported:

> Peter de Havilland and myself went to a dance . . . The mess corporal used to be head waiter at Frascati's and the spread — lobster, crab etc. — was terrific . . . Embry got on to his favourite topic — concentrating on the demoralization of the German flying training organization by means of large numbers of Mosquito long-range intruders operating as an independent unit under his command.

There was nothing new in the technique of night intruding over enemy airfields. Havoc crews of No. 23 Squadron, operating from Ford, had already spread alarm and confusion by stooging stealthily round the bases at which Goering was training and operating his night raiders.

What *was* new at this point was the Mosquito.

Group Captain Embry, the station commander at Wittering, was pressing hard for permission to use the Mosquito as an intruder. Although his request to convert eight Wittering fighters for intruding had been turned down, the Mosquito was in fact emerging elsewhere in this role. Indeed, the intruder crews after their first sampling of a Mosquito came immediately to the conclusion that in their opinion the Mosquito was being wasted as a bomber and as a night fighter.

However, as Embry had already learned to his embitterment, No. 23 Squadron also discovered that there were divided opinions at Fighter Command on the Mosquito's potential as an intruder.

Nevertheless, on 6th July 1942, No. 23 Squadron received their first Mosquito — D.D.670, a night fighter stripped of radar. On the following night the C.O., Wing Commander B. R. O'B. Hoare, set off with Warrant Officer J. F. Potter to prove that the Mosquito would be a first-class intruder aircraft.

It was a hazardous undertaking to fly low-level over enemy territory in the dark and with very limited navigational aid. The more so in an unknown aircraft which had been on the squadron for only a few hours. Near Chartres the intruder spotted a most helpful Dornier 217. The German, believing himself to be safely home, was burning all navigational lights. Three sharp bursts from Hoare — and down in flames went the Mosquito's first victim as an intruder.

Next night it was the turn of Squadron Leader K. M. Salusbury-Hughes to venture forth over France in No. 23 Squadron's first and only Mosquito. In the same area he spotted another luckless Dornier 217 winking its navigation lights invitingly at the Mosquito. After sending the German flaming into the ground from a height of only 1,000 feet, Salusbury-Hughes, delighted with the manoeuvrability and hitting power of D.D.670, looked round for another victim. He could hardly believe his luck when he saw a Heinkel 111. Like the Dornier, the Heinkel was well 'lit up'. The German pilot was circling to land at Evreux when the end of his war came. Salusbury-Hughes set course for home and bed. It had been a satisfactory night's work.

Hoare, Salusbury-Hughes and other intruder pilots at Ford must have smiled when eventually they snuggled down under the blankets after hovering for half the night over enemy territory. Their rooms were in a country house which had been a girls' boarding school before the war. The last thing they saw as they switched off the light was a notice on the wall: 'Ring twice for a mistress'.

By September the enemy were growing wise to the Mosquito intruders, and No. 23 Squadron's pilots were watching carefully for

Wing Commander B. R. O'B. Hoare holds a silver model Mosquito, souvenir of 23 Squadron's hundredth kill — which he scored. He also scored their first.

traps. On 13th September Wing Commander Hoare, spotting the tail light of an enemy aircraft over Twente aerodrome in Holland, assumed it was a decoy to lead him over a concentration of anti-aircraft guns. But instead of attempting to entice the Mosquito over defences, the German suddenly made off. When Wing Commander Hoare used the Mosquito's speed to close on the tail light, the German panicked and flew straight into the ground. D.D.670 had scored another victory without a shot being fired. But Old Faithful was to pay for her luck. On the way home she was hit by flak crossing the enemy coast and Wing Commander Hoare was forced to make a belly landing.

In time, night intruding paid off. The German air training schools in occupied France and the Low Countries were either closed down or moved back.

The Mosquito was fast demonstrating its versatility. By late summer of 1942 the aircraft was operating in four main 'editions': in limited numbers but much in demand on reconnaissance; with misgiving at the top but increasing confidence among the aircrew as a bomber; and on probation as a night fighter and intruder. It was also being considered as a bomber support aircraft, that is a fighter to fly on the fringe of the bomber stream over Germany at night.

In addition, the aeroplane was making a name for itself in a number of smaller and rare editions. For some while there had been mounting impatience over the daylight spying of the Ju 86P, a pressure-cabin unarmed German photographic-reconnaissance aircraft. Ordinarily this aerial spy would have been easy meat for the Hurricane or Spitfire. But at 43,000 feet it remained out of fighting reach of the conventional fighters of the period.

One day in September de Havilland were busy finishing a prototype pressure-cabin bomber, M.P.469, when a Ju 86P hovered over Hatfield with fighters in hot but ineffective pursuit. The Mosquito builders found it particularly galling that there should be an enemy aircraft capable of taking an unchallenged look at their headquarters — especially when they were engaged upon the first pressurized Mosquito.

Seven days later de Havilland had converted M.P.469 into a fighter, extended the wing span, put on smaller wheels and lessened tankage and armour. When M.P.469 took to the air Geoffrey de Havilland climbed her to 43,500 feet.

On their side the RAF made a special contribution to the scheme. A little, lightweight man from No. 151 Squadron appeared at Hatfield to fly the aeroplane, introducing himself as Flying Officer Sparrow.

At the end of this hectic activity the pressure-cabin fighter was not offered much 'trade'. Visits of the Ju 86P became less and less frequent after M.P.469's appearance.

Another small edition was the 'Met' Mosquito. By early autumn 1942, No. 1401 Meteorological Flight possessed two Mosquitos. Like the bomber and recce pilots, the weather men roved unarmed and deep into enemy territory. It was a lonely, dangerous and rather unglamorous occupation.

At about this time, as well, two very surprised members of No. 105 Squadron, Flight Lieutenant Parry and Pilot Officer Robson, were told to report for an operational sortie — in lounge suits. Pilot and navigator were even more amazed when they saw their aircraft. The RAF roundels had vanished, and it no longer carried any numbering or lettering. Crew and aircraft were as incognito as the Air Force would make them. Their object: to run the gauntlet of enemy fighters and deliver a diplomatic bag to the British Embassy in Stockholm.

Parry and Robson reached Stockholm just a few minutes before a German Ju 52 arrived with a load of Goebbels' propaganda staff. That night the two RAF officers enjoyed the wonderful food and the street lighting of the neutral capital. Then, after their night off from rations and the blackout, they flew home with inward Foreign Office despatches, and changed back into uniform.

They had introduced the Mosquito to one of its most adventurous wartime roles. For next year the little wooden aeroplane was to run into its rarest edition — as a 'Bomber in Civies', a courier aircraft flown by BOAC airline Captains.

Wilfrid Freeman, while still Vice Chief of the Air Staff, watched the Mosquito's progress in all these roles with satisfaction. If the bomber version remained, as has been related, unpopular, the Mosquito was greeted with increasing respect in its by-product editions. The problem now was to increase and hasten production; a second de Havilland factory had started on Mosquitos at Leavesden.[1] Canadian-built Mosquitos were on the assembly line in Toronto, but there could be no deliveries until 1943. Plans were being laid to turn the D.H. plant in Australia from Tiger Moth and Dragon building to Mosquito production.

In the meantime delivery of the new Mosquitos came in dribs and drabs, a situation which demanded of Wilfrid Freeman the wisdom of a sort of Air Force Solomon. Much of the responsibility for allotting the available Mosquitos fell upon him. The most persistent Mosquito seeker was Sir Philip Joubert, C-in-C Coastal Command. Week after week, he pleaded for more Mosquitos for the photographic-reconnaissance unit in which Squadron Leader Clerke and Sergeant Sowerbutts had opened the account for the aircraft.

Shortage of photographic-reconnaissance Mosquitos was chronic. Every RAF Command operating the Mosquito, with the exception of Bomber Command, was convinced that every other Command was wasting the new aeroplane. Coastal Command's No. 1 Photographic Reconnaissance Unit was no exception. Repeatedly Joubert, the Coastal C-in-C, stressed that on the long and non-stop Norwegian and German flights to keep a wary eye on the German pocket battleships and cruisers, one Mosquito was capable of doing the work of two Spitfires.

At one point the PRU was down to three Mosquitos operating from Leuchars in Scotland, yet by keeping them in the air the RAF gave the Navy a fairly reasonable service of intelligence.

The value of the Mosquito in this 'edition' can be summed up on one sample sortie over Germany — a flight on which a Mosquito photographed fourteen separate targets including Stettin, Rostock, Lübeck, Bremerhaven, Wilhelmshaven and Emden. The Mosquito's combination of range, endurance and speed, first pioneered in the Comet Races when it won the 1934 England-Australia air race, was making it possible for Britain to take a wide-angle view of Germany and the occupied countries.

They spent their war in a strange world, these recce crews, speeding their Mosquitos among the mares' tails and mackerel skies of the cirrus at 20,000 feet and more, to catch a glimpse which might alter the course of the war, the fate of a convoy.

[1] De Havilland delivered 442 Mosquitos from Hatfield and Leavesden by the end of 1942.

PR.IV DZ383 was a straight conversion from the B.IV, and saw service with 540 Squadron at Benson. It was finally scrapped on 31st October 1946. *(British Aerospace)*

PR.IV DK310 G-LY, flown by Flt Lt Wooll, made an emergency landing at Berne in Switzerland. She was used by Swissair as HB-IMO before going back to the Swiss Air Force as B-5. She was then used as a test-bed for the Swiss Mamba engine circa. 1950, before being declared unserviceable on 9th April 1953.

Seldom did they come home without a picture. Flight Lieutenant Ricketts wrote to Major de Havilland, 'If one has flown 600 miles to a target one doesn't feel like coming home without a picture merely because there is cloud down to 15,000 feet. It all depends on how brave you are feeling at the time.'

Ricketts and his companion Flight Sergeant Boris Lukhmanoff,[1] operating at heights from 25,000 feet, over heavily defended targets, down to 400 feet, obtained some of the war's most magnificent air pictures, including shots of the *Gneisenau* which were issued to the Press and widely published.

Gradually No. 1 PRU became less of a Cinderella unit so far as the delivery of Mosquitos was concerned. On 19th October it rose to Squadron status — No. 540 Squadron, the first photographic-reconnaissance squadron, with fourteen aircraft — and Coastal Command's long-range 'recces' became more commonplace.

There were, of course, losses, including a mishap which put a 'fit' Mosquito out of the war for the duration. Flight Lieutenant G. R. Wooll, who had replaced Ricketts at No. 1 PRU, experiencing engine trouble on a flight to Venice, was obliged to land at Berne in neutral Switzerland. His aircraft, Mosquito D.K.310, spent the remainder of the war under lock and key between two similarly placed Messerschmitts.

The Mosquito was seeing the world. In addition to the home-based P.R. aircraft, three Mosquitos under Flight Lieutenant Sinclair were operating over North Africa from Gibraltar. Towards the end of 1942 one of these aircraft was presented to Colonel Elliott Roosevelt, who commanded an American photographic-reconnaissance unit in North Africa. The majority of Colonel Roosevelt's aircraft were Lockheed Lightnings. After flying his Mosquito, the President's son very soon let it be known that he would willingly exchange a squadron of Lightnings for a squadron of Mosquitos.

Colonel Roosevelt's interest in the Mosquito was to start a ripple of repercussion from the White House through Washington to Whitehall. In Washington, General Arnold had never forgotten the memorable April day when Lord Beaverbrook had taken him to see Geoffrey de Havilland demonstrate W.4050. He began to show a dynamic interest in obtaining Mosquitos for American units. As American desire to operate the Mosquito increased, so did the aeroplane's respectability in the eyes of British air chiefs.

If the Swiss authorities exercised no class distinction in their choice of 'cell mates' for the imprisoned Mosquito, elsewhere in the world of aviation the truth — already so painfully clear to Hermann Goering — began to dawn. 'Freeman's Folly' was an aeroplane in a class of its own.

[1] Until on 11th July 1942 they failed to return from a sortie over Strasburg.

Chapter 8
Low Level and Shallow Dive

The noise of the aeroplane overhead was unfamiliar. It was not the usual heavy drone of four-engine airliners and troop transports. This was the fast-throbbing, exciting, once-heard-never-forgotten roar of two Merlin engines. The diplomatic, military and presidential people of Washington looked up in the watery sunlight of a December day in 1942 and saw their first Mosquito.

In the cockpit, Geoffrey de Havilland was giving a command performance. At the special request of General Arnold, all airport traffic in the vicinity of the federal capital was stilled. For half an hour the British test pilot enjoyed the freedom of the air over Washington in the Canada-built Mosquito he had brought down from Toronto.

The production of a Mosquito in less than a year by de Havilland of Canada is one of the great achievements in the story of aircraft building. In September 1941, when they were most needed at Hatfield, the de Havilland Company despatched Harry Povey, its top production engineer, to Canada with a colleague, W. D. Hunter.[1]

It had been Povey who, in late 1939 and early 1940, had mobilized the woodworking industry to make components for the Mosquito. He rounded up more than 400 sub-contractors, bringing in such unlikely aircraft builders as furniture makers, the Co-op and church pew carvers.

In Toronto, Povey put the same drive into getting the Canada-built Mosquito into production. He scoured North America for suitable machinery. At one critical moment, dollarless and in despair about obtaining a key piece of machinery, he was told of an American engineer named Charles Misfeldt who might be able to help. Misfeldt was in California. Povey flew west and saw him. Misfeldt immediately shipped the necessary machinery to Toronto. It was valued at £40,000, but the American engineer never asked for a penny in payment.

[1] T. C. L. Westbrook, CBE, was de Havilland Production Controller from 1942 to 1945.

Now Geoffrey de Havilland had succeeded in enthralling official America by his demonstration of the Mosquito over Washington.

On the night of the demonstration, General Arnold threw a party for the British pilot and 'Peppy' Burrell, his cockpit companion from Hatfield. The Mosquito was the toast of the air generals. Not until 3 a.m. could de Havilland and Burrell crawl, tired but happy, to bed in their hotel. Before switching off the light an idea occurred to de Havilland. He picked up the bedside telephone: 'Get me my cousin Olivia, in Hollywood,' he said. Pilot and film star were connected. They made a date and the Mosquito was flown west.

The test pilot, who said he really wanted to *see* America, travelled by train.

From Washington, General Arnold began to press, beg and bargain for Mosquito aircraft. At one stage he produced a surprise offer out of Uncle Sam's top hat — Mustangs for Mosquitos. When news of the offer reached Wilfrid Freeman at the Ministry of Aircraft Production, he moved fast to get it turned down. Freeman, who had experienced something of American methods when he accompanied Mr Churchill in the battleship *Prince of Wales* to the Atlantic meeting with President

On board HMS *Prince of Wales*, sailing to the first meeting with Roosevelt, left to right: Admiral Sir Dudley Pound; General Sir John Dill; the Prime Minister and Sir Wilfrid Freeman.

Roosevelt in 1941, feared that such an arrangement would only lead to a series of *quid pro quos*. At the Air Ministry his view was accepted.

In April, Arnold put the heat on. He asked Portal direct for the immediate transfer of twenty-four operational Mosquitos — twelve for the Mediterranean Theatre, twelve to be placed at his disposal at Benson in Britain. In the long term he asked for 235 Mosquitos to equip seven United States photographic-reconnaissance squadrons.

But Portal had no Mosquitos to spare. Although the Americans were to operate Mosquitos in some numbers towards the end of the war, the production position in the spring of 1943 did not allow for such sacrificial aid. Temporarily Portal assuaged Arnold with two Mosquitos for the Middle East.

The U.S. Navy, in spite of its highly individual approach to the requirements of Fleet aircraft, was also covetous of the plywood aeroplane which had been built on the cabbage patch of an English country house. After testing a borrowed Mosquito, the Navy sought 150 machines from Canadian production for night fighting in the Pacific.

Thick and fast the Washington requests for Mosquitos were decoded in Whitehall as they flashed across the Atlantic. It was not possible to accede to them. Total Canadian production for 1943 was to be ninety Mosquitos, and at home the Mosquito was at last earning recognition as a bomber.

From January to June 1943, two crack Mosquito bomber squadrons, Nos. 105 and 139, provided the prick-sharp spearhead of aggression behind which British and American bomber forces were to broaden out the air offensive towards, and beyond, D-Day.

In dry statistical returns of weight of high explosives dropped for targets hit for aircraft lost, the unarmed Mosquito's greatest moments still lay ahead in the 2nd Tactical Air Force and as a member of the Light Night Striking Force. But had the Mosquito no other, or further, contribution to make towards final victory, the glorious record of these squadrons during that period would have more than justified the conception and construction of 'Freeman's Folly'.

Theirs was the most exhilarating and exacting flying job in the Air Force. To fizz in tight formation across the frontiers of Europe called for brilliant airmanship and faultless navigation: wavetop to the enemy coast; up, and over the cliffs, often through a hail of light flak; and on.

First, the fairer suburbs, the Eshers and Surbitons of the enemy. Then the broadening railway tracks, the sooty suburbs. The Maldens, the Clapham Junctions of the Continent. Now, the tall smoky chimneys, grimy signposts pointing the way through the swirling industrial haze to the target for today.

And there it is. A building a peacetime tourist will pass without a glance. But for the two men, elbow to elbow in the tiny cockpit like

In spite of sustaining serious damage, this Mosquito made it home.

spectators at the Cup Final, this is the goal. Behind those smutty brick walls men and women are passing out precision instruments which will help U-boat commanders to drown British seamen and sink British supplies.

Engine sheds, stores depots, small and specialized factories, these were the commonplace targets for the low-level Mosquitos. On occasions they tackled something special, like these two jobs at the end of January.

At the Burmeister and Wain factory in occupied Denmark, the Germans were making U-Boat components. A short, sharp and accurate attack was called for involving a round trip of more than 1,200 miles to Copenhagen. Over the North Sea sped Wing Commander Edwards, leading nine Mosquitos in close formation. Below, the cold, grey-green wavetops licked up at each pregnant bomb belly. In low-level war paint the Mosquitos blended well with sea and countryside. As God plumed his birds to match nature, hunted man had created a jig-saw pattern of dull silvery grey and green on the wings of his aeroplanes.

Low-level unarmed bombers were the special prey of Fw 190 fighters, if they could swoop down from above — and catch them. Danger would intensify over the enemy coast — fighters above, flak below.

Now over the coast. The concentration increases in each cramped cockpit. Edwards checks his landfall. Too far south. Should he press on? Fuel consumption is a vital consideration on this long round trip. Ahead lies Copenhagen and the target. Out there at sea U-Boats are sending British food and materials to the bottom.

The Mosquitos continue on course. One blessing, it is winter. In summer, the windscreens would very soon be smudged with a mash of dust and squashed flies. Suddenly there's a call on the intercom from Flight Lieutenant Gordon: 'I've been hit.' Puffs of blue smoke billow round the starboard wing of his Mosquito. Nobody realizes it at the time but Gordon is now trailing a length of telegraph wire. This *is* low-level attack.

The pilots cannot relax their attention to worry about Gordon. At high speed, at rooftop in tight formation, the risk of collision is ever present. Sometimes it happens. Now the bomb doors are opening. In seconds it is all over. The Mosquitos set course for home. When Edwards lands he has only 15 gallons of fuel in his tanks — enough for about another six and a half miles.

Back at base the crews listened to a German radio report on their day's work. Most of the bombs, the announcer said, were duds. How the airmen laughed. Their bombs, as they knew, were fitted with delayed-action fuses. They could tell to a second what time each bomb would shatter the blackout of Copenhagen. In the bar they toasted each explosion. A round of drinks for each detonation.

Some duds! Some aeroplane!

Three days later came the epic Mosquito air adventure of the year.

Berlin for 'elevenses' and Berlin again for 'tea' — the two daring daylight visits to Hitler's capital which disarranged the carefully prepared celebrations for the tenth anniversary of the Führer's seizure of power. Six aircraft from Nos. 105 and 139 Squadrons were responsible.

The bare details of these attacks have been related at the beginning of this story. In the annals of air bombing the raid is of little account. Scattering a few bombs on the vastness of Berlin could not influence the course of the war. Yet the circumstances in which the Mosquitos arrived over Berlin treated the nation to a good joke. To bomb Berlin at the moment that Goering was about to make an important public and broadcast speech; to bust up the party of the Luftwaffe chief who once boasted that no British aeroplane would ever bomb Germany — and to do just that in daylight; such news came as a tonic to rationed, bombed and war-weary Britain.

There had been keen competition among the Mosquito crews to make the trip. But, once selected, pilots and navigators were not unnaturally a little nervous. Most turned away from the hearty breakfast of tinned orange juice and eggs and bacon served up by the Waafs. This suited one of their number, Flying Officer Wickham. He consumed three tins of orange juice and half a dozen fried eggs. Then he bombed Berlin.

Those who could not take part consoled themselves by tuning the wireless to Berlin. At 11 a.m. their patience was rewarded. The announcer, as he began to introduce Hermann Goering, was interrupted by the crump of an explosion. The speech was postponed for an hour. Flying Officer Wickham and his comrades were bang on.

In war a good national joke is as important a boost for morale as a battle won. It helps to win the next battle. Cheekily the Mosquitos had provided the raw material for a jolly good laugh. The follow-up was swift. That night, after the BBC's ritualistic nine o'clock news, Flying Officer Wickham broadcast an account of his arrival over Berlin. On the Forces' programme a recording of the 'interruption' which delayed Goering's speech was relayed. The Press ran the inevitable stories, epitomized by Sergeant Fletcher's classic remark to a reporter, 'We came out of a cloud and, God bless my soul, there was Berlin!'

The Chief of the Air Staff received the crews. There were decorations all round. The DSO for Squadron Leader R. W. Reynolds, DFC's for the other officers, DFM's for the sergeants.

To cap it all, Lord Haw-Haw helped to make a good joke even better.

'Thanks to the U-Boat campaign,' he smirked, 'Britain is so starved of materials that she has been compelled to build her bombers of wood.'

Low Level and Shallow Dive. These were the two forms of attack which were giving undying glory to the name Mosquito. When low level and shallow dive were combined in an assault by one small force of Mosquitos on one target the results would be devastating. While the first

Was this what was meant by 'a wing and a prayer'? What else but the Mossie could take this kind of punishment?

formation bombed with eleven-second fuses from a height of 0-50 feet, the second formation shallow-dive bombed with instantaneous fuses from 1,500 feet in the wake of the low-levellers. This procedure was dangerous in the extreme and called for precision flying and expert navigation. The last Mosquito to shallow-dive had to be clear of the target before the bombs from the first Mosquito exploded. Only targets of the utmost importance were selected for the professional attention of Nos. 105 and 139 Squadron crews employing this precise technique in daylight.

One such target, the molybdenum mine at Knaben in South Norway, was bombed on 3rd March 1943. Ten crews from No. 139 Squadron were selected for the job. It was an opportunity, they were told, to aim a heavy blow at Germany's steel alloy industry. Much of the plant had been supplied by America before the war, and could not be replaced easily. Despite Fw 190 interceptions, not a bomb was wasted. Washing, flotation and crushing plants were demolished. Next day a fire broke out in the drill-repairing sheds. Seventy new drills and many old ones were destroyed. The price paid: one Mosquito, crewed by Flying Officer A. N. Bulpitt and Sergeant K. A. Amond, who fell to a Focke-Wulf fighter.

Another Mosquito, piloted by Flying Officer J. H. Brown, was badly damaged but flew home to demonstrate the amount of punishment the wooden aeroplane could take. This machine landed with no hydraulics to operate the undercarriage, no air speed indicator, no rudder controls and no elevator trim. Six days later Brown underwent a similar experience after taking part in a 16-Mosquito attack on engine sheds at Le Mans.

But low-level and shallow-dive attacks, though rewarding in terms of destruction, remained tremendously dangerous. They brought profit — and loss. Pertinaciously the crack No. 105 and No. 139 Squadron crews carried out attack after attack and there were many lucky escapes, like Brown's. But the luck did not always stick to one pilot and finally Brown was among those who 'bought it'. His Mosquito, D.Z.470, maimed by coastal flak on the way to bomb engine sheds at Malines, was finished off three minutes later by two Fw 190's.

The two Mosquito bomber squadrons exploited the versatility of their aircraft. The low-level day raids were interspersed with high-level night visits to Berlin. These nocturnal sorties were equally adventurous. Moonlit, fine, cloudless nights — the most dangerous nights — were chosen for the Mosquitos. In the early summer of 1943 navigational facilities in the tiny cockpit were limited. It helped the crews to pick their way to Berlin if they could see the landmarks until the glinting Havel and Tegel lakes to the west of the city told them that they had arrived.

An uncanny emotional relationship was now building up between the Mosquito crews and their aircraft. The Mosquito was a loved aeroplane. The sentiment that welled up inside the men whose lives depended on

Mk. II HJ920 joined 25 Squadron on 22nd November 1942, remaining with the squadron until 20th January 1944 when, due to undercarriage problems, its pilot force-landed at Acklington, Northumberland. HJ920 was later written off as spares. *(via Stuart Howe)*

Wing Commander John Wooldridge, composer and Mosquito pilot.

the Mosquito amounted to something more than an airman's professional regard for an aeroplane's graceful lines, smooth handling and mechanical efficiency. This was a truly emotional attachment which would prompt a whole squadron to solemnly stand round a Mosquito with an outstandingly fine operational record and drink a toast to the aeroplane. For no apparent reason ground crews would also fall in love with particular Mosquitos. There was, for instance, 'Romanita', or Mosquito 529 of No. 25 Squadron, which was given preferential treatment and cosseted by the fitters. 'Romanita' was also much sought after by the pilots. When her regular 'driver', Flight Lieutenant J. F. R. Jones, was on leave, other pilots in the squadron drew lots to fly her.

Wing Commander John de L. Wooldridge, the composer, was moved to pay this tribute to the Mosquito during the period when he commanded No. 105 Squadron and led many of the low-level day and high-level night attacks in early 1943. Writing to Major de Havilland, he said:

> The Mosquito bomber is, in every way, an outstanding aeroplane — easy to fly, highly manoeuvrable, fast and completely free from vices of any sort. From our point of view, it has a further quality, a highly important one in wartime — and that is an extraordinary capacity for taking a knocking about. Owing to the high speed and rooftop height at which defended areas are crossed, the Mosquito very often tends to be immune from flak, but there are, of course, occasions when someone 'cops a packet'.
>
> I myself had an experience of this kind a short time ago. While approaching a target at approximately 100 feet above the ground, with the bomb doors open, my aircraft was hit by three Bofors shells. Apart from the distinct thud as the shells exploded and a rather unpleasant smell of petrol, the behaviour of the aircraft after impact appeared to be normal and the bombs were dropped successfully. Actual damage was as follows. The first shell entered the lower surface of the port mainplane, approximately four feet from the wing tip, and burst inside, removing three square feet of the upper wing surface. The aileron was fortunately undamaged. The second shell hit the port engine nacelle fairly far back, wrecking the undercarriage retraction gear, severing the main oil pipe line, damaging the airscrew pitch control and putting the instruments on the blind flying panel out of action. The third shell entered the fuselage just in front of the tail plane and severed the tail wheel hydraulic line and the pressure head line, rendering the air speed indicator useless. After a while, on the way home, the port engine began to give trouble and eventually it failed. Although the airscrew could not be feathered, a ground speed of almost 200 m.p.h. was maintained on the return journey and the aircraft was landed in

pitch darkness on its belly without the assistance of flaps.

There have been other notable examples. On one occasion a Mosquito went through a set of high tension cables which appeared unexpectedly in the target area, but returned to its base slightly bent, and was landed on the wheels in the dark without further damage. Another machine was severely damaged on its run-up, one engine was put out of action and the bomb-release gear failed. This Mosquito was brought home safely on one engine with all the bombs on board, flying only a few feet above the sea, and made a successful belly landing at night. The pilot reported that the machine 'had been a bit sluggish, but worked all right'. Yet another machine had its elevator controls severed, but was brought home controlled fore and aft purely by means of the flaps and throttles!

The aeroplane flies so well on one engine that the opinion in this Squadron (105) is that the de Havilland Company must have originally designed it as a single-engined aeroplane, and then stuck another one on for luck. It is entirely free from unpleasant vices at all times, which is a great factor when making night landings when damaged, and owing to the clean design of the underside, it can in emergency be landed on its belly with very little damage, an important factor when considering serviceability. All round, it is a sturdy, pugnacious little brute, but thoroughly friendly to its pilot.

In conclusion, the Mosquito represents all that is finest in aeronautical design. It is an aeroplane that could only have been conceived in this country and combines the British genius for building a practical and straightforward machine with the typical de Havilland flair for producing a first-rate aeroplane that looks right and *is* right.

The Mosquito chose its own and very charming way of thanking Wing Commander Wooldridge for this tribute. In May 1944, shortly before reducing the transatlantic record to five hours and forty minutes in a West-East Mosquito flight, Wooldridge visited the United States, where he met Artur Rodzinski, conductor of the New York Philharmonic Orchestra.

For weeks past, on his moonlight missions over Germany, the pilot had found inspiration for a symphonic poem on the wonders and mysteries of the constellations as seen through the eyes of a bomber pilot. Rodzinski agreed to perform the work in New York — 'A Solemn Hymn for Victory' by Wing Commander J. de L. Wooldridge, DFC and bar, DFM.[1]

The month of June 1943, as will be seen, was to usher in a new phase of the Mosquito Bomber's career. Meanwhile, in the last days of May,

[1] Wing Commander Wooldridge died on 27th October 1958, after a motor accident.

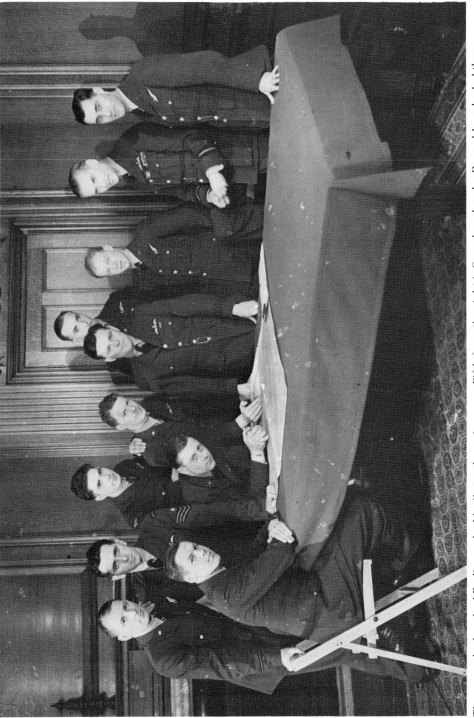

The men who bombed Berlin on the Nazi's tenth anniversary. Fifth from the right is Squadron Leader Reynolds, who led them.

plans were perfected for the final major daylight low-level operation by Nos. 105 and 139 Squadrons. They were to attack the Schlott Glass Works and the Zeiss Optical Instrument Works at Jena, 45 miles from Leipzig.

There follows the personal account of Wing Commander Reynolds, who led the fourteen Mosquitos which took part in the raid. It is repeated as written by the Wing Commander after his hazardous journey on 27th May 1943.

I was leading in B for Beer, No. D.Z.601, a particularly fine Mossie . . . We formed up in the circuit area of the airfield and then set course on what was to be the deepest low-level daylight penetration we have yet undertaken, and also one of the most eventful — for me, anyway.

The North Sea was crossed at wavetop height and on approaching the enemy coast, always the most tense moment, speed was increased and the formation closed up for the quick dash across. Once over, the trip becomes more interesting. One sees such things as cyclists jumping off their cycles to have a look round to see what is coming. Children look up at us, then put their heads down and run as hard as they can.

Frequently one has narrow squeaks with birds — an enemy of the low-flying aircraft. If they do hit the kite serious damage is almost sure to be caused.

There were no further incidents until we ran over one of Germany's reservoirs, when the Hun pushed up some accurate flak at us. Fortunately no one was hit but shortly afterwards two of the formation collided and crashed. It was another 50 miles or so further on when bad weather was encountered. Firstly, thick industrial haze and then heavy low clouds covering the tops of the hills over which we had to fly. Of course we had to enter cloud and climb to safety height, i.e. high enough to clear the hills with a margin of safety. As soon as we estimated that we should have cleared the high hills, we descended into the gloom beneath the clouds.

To enable the other chaps to pick me up again, a very difficult job under the existing weather conditions, I put on my navigation lights for a short while. This was also done by the leader of the second section, Squadron Leader Blessing. Crews afterwards stated that this was a great help for them to regain formation.

At this stage we had arrived at a point approximately 20 miles from the target and we turned to our run-up, increasing speed and then opening bomb doors. We picked up various landmarks which we were looking for, and knew from these that we were dead on track. The visibility was now down to about 1,500 yards — not much when one is travelling at such high speed.

The target was now only two miles away but not yet in sight. At a thousand yards I picked up the tall chimneys and opened up to full throttle. My observer pointed out the balloons, and immediately the flak came up at us in bright red streams and unhealthily close. I could see one gun on a flak tower firing away as hard as he could at someone on my right. Now it was every man for himself. I picked out a tall building and went for it, releasing my bombs at point-blank range, yanked the stick back to climb over the building, and as I topped it, the airscrew received a direct hit. There was a violent explosion in front of my eyes and I felt something tug at my hand and leg but took no notice for the time being. Things were too hot.

Now we were in a veritable hail of tracer shells, dodging and twisting for dear life. More balloons ahead, which we missed by the Grace of God, and now, apart from a few inaccurate bursts, we were clear and I was able to survey the damage.

My left hand was bleeding freely, as was my left leg. The kite was vibrating considerably and I could see holes in the fairing immediately in front of the radiator. Flak had pierced a hole just aft of the port radiator and close to one of the main tanks. There were two large holes in the fuselage close to the throttle box, where some fittings had been blown away. My intercom had packed up and I discovered later that a splinter had severed the lead just below my starboard ear. The collar of my battledress was torn too. This wasn't noticed until I arrived back at base, when Flight Lieutenant Sismore, my navigator, asked me what I had done to get that.

However, to continue. After that one violent explosion it seemed a miracle that the aircraft could keep in the air. I was especially anxious about my port radiator with that hole so near and constantly checked the temps to watch for any rise. Fortunately it remained constant at 97°C and the vibrating got no worse, so the need to feather the damaged propeller never arose.

We were now returning individually, and so I nipped into the low cloud for safety — to clear hills and avoid any flak that may have been put up. My observer bound up my hand and then we settled down to the long journey home with a frequent apprehensive glance at the engine instruments and fuel. I personally felt satisfied that I got the target with my bombs and later one of the boys said that he saw them go in, followed by a sheet of flame a hundred feet high — and it would be some time before they actually exploded.

On the way back we ran into more trouble by entering two more defended areas. The second one was very hot and it was with luck that we escaped by means of violent evasive action combined with full throttle and fine pitch.

From now on the return journey was uneventful. Petrol was

Wing Commander Reynolds, leader of the Berlin raid, discusses another raid on his return, wounded by a piece of wood the size of a grapefruit shot out of his propeller.

A trio of B.XVIs on the tarmac being bombed up and serviced ready for the evening sortie. *(Flight International)*

checked and we decided that we should have sufficient. On arrival back at base we discovered that there was not much left. But our worries were over now so we did not bother any more.

Even though B for Beer was badly damaged she behaved magnificently throughout and is now being repaired, which will take a few days. One of the port engine bearers had a large hole through the middle of it but the vital parts of the engine were sound.

Three of the fourteen Mosquitos which set out for Jena failed to return. Two more were written off while attempting to land. Their crews perished.

The achievement of the unarmed, and formerly unwanted, wooden speed bomber did not escape the notice of the C-in-C, Bomber Command. Air Marshal Harris now discovered that he could do with more Mosquito aircraft, to bomb in their own right and to light the way for his heavies.

Group Captain Bennett introduced the wooden aeroplane to his new

Pathfinder Force. A first squadron of 'musical' Mosquitos was formed —
No. 109 Squadron — so called because they were equipped with a new
radio blind-bombing device called Oboe.

With delight Major de Havilland reported to his brother:

> Thanks to the magnificent job 105 and 139 Squadrons have done
> during the past four months, the bomber version has taken on a
> new lease of life. Even the C-in-C Bomber Command knows of its
> existence, but this is mainly due to its activities as Pathfinder for the
> heavies . . . Air Marshal Harris told me that he had, quite frankly,
> been surprised at the success Mosquitos had had on low-level
> attacks and said as much in a letter he addressed to the units
> concerned. But he still considers that only a very small force should
> be diverted from the normal bombing routine for this type of work.
> For Pathfinding, which, he stated, will become the most important
> of all duties, the Mosquito is indispensable.

The little wooden aeroplane had earned esteem with Air Marshal
Harris, the most exacting of bombing masters. Now he called for more
and more Mosquitos. He asked Freeman about the prospects of future
production and he wrote to Portal with a strong recommendation that
production be increased, as the position was very unsatisfactory.

The Mosquitos of No. 109 Squadron having very soon demonstrated
the aeroplane's suitability in its new application as a Pathfinder for the
heavy bombers, Nos. 105 and 139 Squadrons were also earmarked to join
Bennett's famous force. When the news of this impending change of
occupation reached the crews they were disconsolate. They had come to
relish the dangerous activities of their daylight role.

No less put out were some of their former comrades who, with eight
aircraft, had already been diverted from daylight operations to train with
Coastal Command for yet another application of the Mosquito. As Major
de Havilland reported at the time, 'They raised hell about this, but to no
effect.' They would have raised even greater hell had they known then
that the job for which they were diverted, and were to train so long and
so arduously, was eventually to be rendered unnecessary by the advent
of a new weapon in air warfare — the atom bomb. For the eventual task
for which these RAF Mosquitos were selected was to take off from two
aircraft carriers and attack the Imperial Japanese Fleet with Barnes
Wallis's dam-busting bouncing bombs!

Chapter 9
Postmen and Pathfinders

In the last days of 1942 a well-built, wavy-haired Wing Commander, who had joined the RAF in peacetime as a boy aircraft apprentice, carried the sting of the Mosquito to the Mediterranean. Over Christmas, Wing Commander P. G. Wykeham-Barnes led No. 23 Squadron — the first Mosquito intruder specialists — by way of Algiers and Gibraltar to the island of Malta.

From 29th December, when Wykeham-Barnes flew the first Mosquito intruder sortie off the island, there followed a period remarkable for the Mosquito crews' sustained aggression. In their first month No. 23 Squadron flew 184 operational sorties. These included 73 intruder patrols and 82 attacks on ground targets. The Mosquito also carried out 27 patrols in co-operation with the torpedo aircraft. They terrorized the Axis from the Sicilian airfields to Pantellaria, Naples, Taranto, Tunis and Bizerta. They roamed the blue skies of the Mediterranean. They beat up trains. They harassed the enemy's road transport between Tripoli and Sfax. Intruding over enemy air bases, they reduced fighter interference with RAF and naval reconnaissance, bombing and torpedo operations.

Their favourite activity was to panic enemy airfields at night and then retire to a respectful distance and watch the flak defences pumping away at the enemy's own aircraft — or at nothing. Buccaneers of the blue skies, they soon earned their popular name: The Malta Pirates.

Wykeham-Barnes, the Pirate captain, was a great intruder enthusiast. He worked his crews hard. He believed in relentless pressure on the enemy from the air and plenty of exercise and P.T. on the ground to keep his Mosquito crews fit, operationally and physically. The former enthusiasm proved disastrous to the enemy. The latter sometimes rebounded on the Pirates. On 2nd April 1943, to quote No. 23 Squadron's Operations Record Book, Pilot Officer E. Pullen 'disintegrated himself' in the eliminating heats of the sports by entering for several

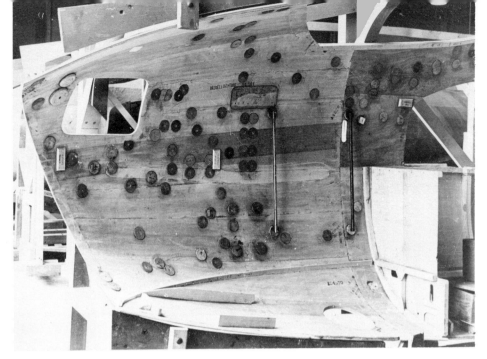

In this picture the small plywood discs, or ferrules, can be clearly seen which were used for the attachment of fittings. *(British Aerospace)*

Wings under construction at William Birch's factory at High Wycombe, August 1943. *(British Aerospace)*

events. Alighting in the long jump sandpit, the Pilot Officer 'pancaked with his undercart up'.

Three weeks later, on the day after Wykeham-Barnes's DSO had been announced, it was reported to the Engineer Officer that the C.O. had 'damaged himself'. The Engineer's immediate reaction was to establish the state of operational fitness of the C.O.'s Mosquito. Rushing off to inspect the aeroplane, he saw a large and familiar figure hobbling along on crutches. It was a much relieved Engineer Officer who learned the details of the Wing Commander's 'damage'. He had torn a cartilage tossing a ball to Group Captain Miller, the station commander. His Mosquito was intact. Engineer Officers on Mosquito squadrons in early 1943 knew that a C.O. was the more readily replaceable than the Wooden Wonder.

Wykeham-Barnes was flown home for repair in a Dakota — to earn new renown later taking part in some of the most daring and successful Mosquito low-level attacks on pinpoint targets in Europe. In the meantime, after introducing the Mosquito to the Mediterranean war, the Wing Commander hobbled into Major de Havilland's office at Hatfield for a chat and a cup of tea.

A few weeks later Hereward de Havilland set off to make a personal inspection of Mosquitos in the Mediterranean and the Middle East. He was flown out in a Liberator of Transport Command. In case of an accident he was handed a note written in Arabic, which said that the British Government would pay quite a lot for him if delivered whole, but practically nothing if chopped up. Major de Havilland reported to his company:

'Air Vice Marshal Dawson, Chief Maintenance and Supply Officer of Mediterranean Air Command, arranged facilities for me to go anywhere and see more or less anything. Dawson is an outstanding personality and was sent out from England by Beaverbrook as a result of Eden's 1941 report that the RAF maintenance and supply organization in the Middle East was in a mess. Given carte blanche, he ruthlessly scrapped inefficient methods and officers and put the show on a proper footing, just in time.'

At Boufarik, inland from Algiers, Mosquito repairs were being undertaken in a French tobacco factory. 'The director', de Havilland wrote, 'is a Frenchman, Camas, who was a senior technical officer of Caudron-Renault in Paris. He got out with about fifty of their best men just before the Germans arrived, and set up the show at Boufarik.'

Major de Havilland flew on to Malta from Algiers in a Bisley. On the way, as he was much too hot, he painted the inside of the cockpit with metal polish to keep the sun out.

'We landed at Luqa', he continued, 'where to our astonishment we were immediately given free cups of tea by Transport Command. Wing Commander Selby, DSO, DFC, who took over No. 23 Squadron from

A PR.XVI of 60 Squadron (South African Air Force). *(SAAF)*

Wykeham-Barnes, showed me round Luqa and talked much of Mosquitos overheating. He is larger than Wykeham-Barnes, rather like Claud Dampier, and used to be a BBC announcer . . .

'The detachment of No. 256 Squadron which went to Malta under Squadron Leader Allan in July have done wonderfully well with their Mark VIII A.I. Mosquitos. When I was there, the total of enemy aircraft destroyed was twenty-eight, of which Allan himself has got fourteen.'[1]

Next, Major de Havilland left Malta in the Bisley to try and locate Colonel Roosevelt and his Mosquitos at La Maza near Tunis.

'A mild dust storm was on at La Maza,' he wrote. 'There were two Me 109's upside down in bomb craters and a burnt-out Ju 88 just off the landing strip. After walking 1½ miles I discovered "No. 10 Mosquito Special Task Force, Photographic" in an E.P. tent with Major Phillip A. Kennedy in charge.'

The Mosquito envoy discovered that Roosevelt was in America and his unit was now without a single Mosquito. Major de Havilland continued, 'From La Maza we went to Ariana, a few miles west, to see B flight of No. 60 Squadron, SAAF. There they were under canvas and had one Mark VI Mosquito which they use for training. This is a photographic unit and they have been told they are getting twelve Mark IX aircraft. Over a lunch of bully beef and dust they rhapsodized about the Mosquito and told how they had done the Mareth Line photography on the first two Mark II's to arrive in Africa, both of which are now written off . . . Their main grouse was complete lack of activity. They have never had a Mosquito jack and have therefore never once done a hydraulic or undercarriage retraction test.

---

[1] This officer, flying a Mosquito, shot down 10 enemy aircraft in one week during July 1943. On 15th July he created a night-fighter record by not only destroying 5 enemy aircraft in one night, but accounting for each of them during the same patrol.

Next day de Havilland lunched with Tedder at Algiers. Tedder said he wanted more photographic-reconnaissance Mosquitos badly, and some long-range fighters.

In Egypt, during his tour, Major de Havilland inspected a depot where Merlins were being repaired in caves from which the ancient Egyptians had cut the stones for the Pyramids. He also called on BOAC, who were operating, among other aircraft, the de Havilland Flamingo.

At home BOAC had also become a Mosquito customer, flying a fast Mosquito courier service to Stockholm, where BOAC Captains delivered *The Times*, Savile Row suits and Lincoln Bennett hats for businessmen and industrialists who were helping our war effort. For the return journey the 'bombers in civvies' loaded up with ball bearings and precision instruments.

They also carried people.

Crouched in the bomb bay, sometimes two at a time, the BOAC 'passengers' sped high across the sea, knowing nothing of the outside world until the bomb doors opened — and out they tumbled on to the tarmac.

Delivered in Scotland or Sweden as breathing parcels wrapped up in two flying suits, Mae West and parachute harness, the passengers were unpacked and revealed as diplomats, industrialists, bishops, musicians, professors and cloak-and-dagger experts. Out of one parcel stepped Sir Malcolm Sargent; from another Dr Bell, Bishop of Chichester.

One of the BOAC Mosquitos. *(via Stuart Howe)*

A fine shot of B.XVI ML963. *(Charles E. Brown)*

A *Daily Telegraph* correspondent who made the journey wrote, 'Riding across the North Sea is like squeezing into a tiny ice box and crouching there stiffly for several hours without any real sense of motion or altitude despite the fact that no civilian passenger ever flew so fast, so high before.'

The BOAC Captains were worked hard and a number lost their lives. On one night early in 1944, Captain J. H. White flew three trips to Stockholm and back.

BOAC Mosquitos also carried the Royal Mail for the GPO and much prisoner-of-war mail was exchanged on this route. Women travelled too, so that nobody was surprised to see Lady Mallet, wife of the wartime Minister to Sweden, being handed out of the bomb racks with the diplomatic bags.

Some of the Luftwaffe crews, who by this time were hearing from their homes, as prisoners-of-war, by way of the BOAC Mosquito mail carriers, had been shot down while they were taking a leaf out of the Mosquito intruder's book. Enemy Me 410 intruders came in with RAF bomber formations returning from Germany, tagging along like gatecrashers at a party. On the principle of 'set a thief to catch a thief', the Mosquitos were employed to hunt them out. The Me 410 presented a particularly difficult problem, as in silhouette it resembled the Mosquito, and its pilots often operated with as much daring as their opposite numbers.

Special measures were needed, and early in 1944 Wing Commander John Cunningham introduced the 'pep pill' Mosquito to night fighting in No. 85 Squadron. This version employed a system of nitrous oxide injection which gave a night-fighter pilot an increase of nearly 50 m.p.h. at 28,000 feet for several minutes. On the night of 2nd January 1944, flying a 'pep pill' Mosquito operationally Cunningham bagged an Me 410.

No. 85 Squadron, which had earned much day renown earlier in the war under Wing Commander Peter Townsend, took an especially heavy

78

toll of German night raiders with their Mosquitos, but the crews had some narrow squeaks. One night John Cunningham escaped with glass splinters in the face and eyes when three bullets from a Ju 88 cracked his Mosquito's bullet-proof windscreen.

Commanding the squadron, Cunningham and his navigator, Squadron Leader Rawnsley, accounted for 4 raiders as a Mosquito crew. Squadron Leader Burbridge and Flight Lieutenant Skelton shot down 20 raiders — all at night, including a bag of four in a night — leaving them one short of Squadron Leader Allan's Mosquito record at Malta.

No. 85 Squadron's final war bag was 278 enemy aircraft, 168 of which were shot down at night. Of these 67 were over Britain and 67 over Germany in support of heavy bombers.

Bomber Command's losses were mounting. Harnessed elbow to elbow above a blazing Germany, Mosquito crews watched bomber upon bomber fall flaming, each a flying tinder box, into the furnace of its own kindling.

Comforted by the surge of power in the Rolls-Royce engine to port and starboard of their compact little night world of flickering needles, and feeling the more secure by virtue of their speed and manoeuvrability, the Mosquito crews broadened their activities in order to help the heavy bombers.

Fussily, attentively, they nursemaided the main bomber force to and from Germany. Mosquitos sampled the weather ahead of the great droning formations of Lancaster, Stirling and Halifax bombers. They ranged occupied Europe to seek out, listen to and counter enemy radio and radar devices of air defence. They intruded over enemy air bases to prevent night fighters from taking off. Painfully aware of the vulnerability of the ponderous four-engine bombers, the Mosquito squadrons also provided escorts for them, engaging enemy defenders in moonlit dog-fights over their home ground. The Mosquito pilots, many of whom had participated in the night fighter protection of London, looked upon their new role in support of the heavy bombers over German targets as the most valuable contribution they could make to the growing assault.

No. 85 Squadron were among those who joined the special bomber support Group of Mosquitos — No. 100 Group. In the Group's 'Review of Operations' this Squadron reported:

> Flying high we had the added perk of witnessing night after night the most stupendous avalanche of fireworks that made the pre-war Crystal Palace and Blackpool rolled into one look like a damp squib.
>
> Our first high-level success was on September 11th, when Squadron Leader Burbridge and Flight Lieutenant Skelton launched out again on their outstanding life of midnight murder — destroying a Ju 88.

No. 239 Squadron, operating in the same Group, wrote:

> Many low-level intruder patrols were flown but the general opinion was that an occasional squirt at a truck or a train was poor excitement by comparison with the full-blooded thrill of an A.I.[1] chase terminating in the destruction of a Hun.

Not all Mosquito crews would agree that low-level intruding was an unexciting occupation. Marking for the heavy bombers, and intruding — each produced its own brand of 'excitement'.

Flying Officer L. Holliday of No. 105 Squadron caught such a packet marking for a force of twenty-five other Mosquitos attacking Leverkusen that, on his return, the NCO in charge of the Mosquito on the ground likened the peppered aeroplane to a colander.

Incidentally, there was always the risk in intruding that a Mosquito's pilot's own daring would involve his aeroplane in the wreckage of a victim. Flight Lieutenant M. A. Cybulski and Flying Officer H. H. Ladbrook of No. 410 Squadron had made contact with a Do 217 over its base. Closing to 100 feet the pilot gave a three-secondburst of cannon fire. The Dornier exploded, but burning petrol and oil flew back on to the Mosquito, scorching the fuselage from nose to tail. Parts of both wings were singed, the rudder fabric was torn away, and the port engine was put out. In the cockpit, Cybulski, blinded by the flash of the explosion, could not read his instruments and the Mosquito went into a steep dive, losing 4,000 feet before the dive miraculously extinguished the fire. At this point, Ladbrook seized the stick and kept the scorched aircraft under control until Cybulski could see again. After staggering home, Cybulski and Ladbrook realized how nearly they had become the victims of their own audacity.

Squadron Leader Moran and Flight Sergeant Rogers of No. 418 Squadron were over an enemy airfield when they spotted a bomber waiting to land. The Mosquito opened fire and the enemy blew up in Moran's face. The Squadron Leader pulled the stick back and felt a terrific jolt as the cockpit filled with smoke. Thinking the aeroplane was on fire, he told Rogers to bale out. In the confusion Rogers did not get the order and shortly afterwards Moran regained control and decided to try and fly home.

Over the sea the port engine caught fire. As the flames spread to the wing, the pilot again ordered the navigator to jump. Rogers left with some difficulty, the bottom hinge of the door jamming as he tried to jettison it. When Moran tried to get out of his seat, part of his harness got caught. As he struggled to free himself, the Mosquito went out of control, losing height to about 1,000 feet above the waves. He sat in his seat again and pulled the stick back. The Mosquito rocketed up, port

---

[1] Radar-guided Air Interception.

wing down. Squadron Leader Moran then managed to clear himself, and keeping his right hand on the stick as long as possible he turned on his stomach and slid out of the aircraft feet first.

He was picked up by an Air-Sea Rescue launch.

Certainly intruding was considered sufficiently hazardous, whatever the opinion of the fighter crews, for superstition to creep into many an intruder cockpit in the shape of mascots or the observance of lucky ritual.

Squadron Leader Mack, a New Zealand member of No. 25 Squadron, never flew without a picture of Susan, his six-months-old daughter, in the cockpit. Mack's fellow pilots knew this and when the Squadron Leader was 'off ops', succeeding 'drivers' asked if they might keep the picture in the Mosquito. Susan's luck brought her father home on one occasion with four feet sliced off the starboard wing.

Bombing by Mosquito also brought its quota of close shaves. Sergeant S. F. Parlato, a pilot of No. 139 Squadron in Bennett's Pathfinder Force, was a 'press-on' type. Making his first trip as a member of a diversionary attack by eight Mosquitos on Oldenburg while the main force was bombing Hanover, Parlato, as the Ops Book records, was 'not content with the small fires at Oldenburg, and went on to bomb Hanover with the main force'.

Three nights later Parlato and his navigator, Sergeant D. D. Thomas, encountered heavy flak over Düsseldorf — but came home again safely. The following night Parlato and Thomas were out once more — the target, Hamborn. Two minutes before the bombs were released their Mosquito was hit. A piece of flak smashed the P.4 Compass and wounded Parlato just above the knee. As the bombs went whistling down into Germany, the Mosquito was hit again — this time in the nacelle of the starboard engine. Once more the Mosquito saw the wounded pilot home. Maintenance mended the Mosquito and Parlato was repaired at the RAF Hospital, Ely. A month later both returned to ops.

Squadron Leader G. H. Wilson, flying as navigator to Flying Officer J. R. Cassels in a Mosquito raid on Ludwigshafen, had a particularly lucky escape. After the aircraft had been hit the navigator felt up to his goggles for the pencil which he normally carried there, much as a grocer's ear serves the same purpose. But the pencil had gone — whipped off Wilson's head and out of the cockpit by a fragment of flak.

It was not exceptional for Mosquito pilots to press on to another target as Sergeant Parlato did — even if they were by that time bombless.

After a raid on Lübeck, No. 139 Squadron recorded that 'All crews bombed in the face of heavy searchlight activity and moderate flak . . . Some stayed to watch the Hamburg raid and found it very spectacular.'

Which says a great deal for the confidence inspired in aircrews throughout the Royal Air Force by a little wooden aeroplane, built in a garden behind a moat, and ordered unseen off the drawing-board.

Chapter 10
Embry and the Pinpoint Raids

The personality of the Mosquito and a reflection of the aircrews' confidence in it was mirrored even in official forms. The ruled sheets, Forms 540 and 541, on which RAF squadrons record their monthly and daily operational activities contain some heady stuff.

In new Mosquito squadrons there was always great excitement about the impending arrival of the aircraft. For instance, on 21st October 1943, No. 25 Squadron had declared: 'A memorable day for the squadron. To the delight of all, it was made known this morning that we were to be re-equipped with de Havilland Mosquito aircraft. A few minutes later the first three arrived on the aerodrome.' The entry ended with a remark ascribed to an American signals officer on the station:

'Gee, they must be fast ships. They've nearly beaten the rumour!'

No. 605 Squadron noted that a 'book' had been opened on the delivery prospects of a first Mosquito. Odds of five to one against delivery by the following February were laid in November 1942. The subject of the betting touched down on the second day of February 1943. 'Form' dictated changes in the betting. Eggs, the special ration for operational aircrew, had only to be heard sizzling for breakfast, and the market would fall dramatically. A first Mosquito for No. 239 Squadron arrived on 31st December 1943 — nine days after eggs appeared on the breakfast table.

The New Zealanders of No. 487 Squadron filled in their forms with an almost feverish intensity when Mosquitos were in the offing. 'Two Mosquitos should have arrived today. Perhaps tomorrow.' (20th August 1943.) And next day: 'Here they come! Just two today — bags of excitement.'

Then, 'The Mossies that arrived last night have been exercised fairly hard all day today in glorious weather. It is a pretty aircraft. The squadron is generally as pleased as a child with a new toy.' And on 26th

Loading the Mosquito's heaviest bomb, the 4,000-pounder.

August: 'All anybody talks about here is Mosquitos.' Finally, on 5th September: 'The Vents (Venturas) are gradually going and these beautiful, graceful little grey machines taking their places.'

Like all Mosquito squadrons, No. 487 worked single-mindedly to become operational in their new twin-engined aircraft. After the sweat of conversion from Venturas the aircrews rewarded the ground crews with a beer party for their exertions.

Operational again, the New Zealanders missed no opportunity to attack the enemy. On the last day of 1943, when the squadron moved from Sculthorpe to Hunsdon, the Mosquitos flew to their new base via 'targets' in the Pas de Calais — and arrived at Hunsdon in time for a beer before lunch.

They felt in particularly good form, these Kiwis, for the King had recently approved their design for a squadron crest. This was a Teko-Teko,[1] symbolic of the Maori fighting spirit, carved in wood and holding a bomb coloured in gold. The motto: *Ki Te Mutunga* — 'Through to the End'.

[1] A grotesque carved Maori figure, depicted in an attitude of defiance and brandishing a weapon. It was fixed above the entrance to the *whare-whakairo*, or meeting house of the tribe.

Nos. 21 and 464 (Royal Australian Air Force) Squadrons also bombed targets en route for their new base when they moved to Hunsdon. These targets were V1 launching sites, under construction but not yet in action. Revealed previously by Mosquito photographic reconnaissance over Peenemünde, Hitler's Revenge Weapons might well have turned the tide of war decisively, had it not been for the audacity and accuracy of Mosquito crews in low-level and shallow-dive attacks.

This is what Air Chief Marshal Sir Philip Joubert has to say[1] about the air strikes against the V1 and V2:

> If the efforts of Colonel Wachtel, in charge of V1 bombardment and Commanding Officer of the special Flak Regiment 155W, had not been interfered with and Hitler's intention to fire 5,000 V1's every 24 hours had borne fruit, some 600,000 flying bombs would have been launched against Britain between June and September 1944. In fact only 5,430 were discharged, causing 6,100 deaths and injury to 17,300 people. Approximately one million houses were destroyed or damaged in Greater London. If the 600,000 V1's had arrived at their

[1] In his book *Rocket* (Hutchinson, 1956).

A typical scene with the ground crew waiting to load up an FB.VI of 487 Squadron (RNZAF) with its 500 pounders. *(Stuart Howe)*

An Australian Mosquito in flight over southern England in September 1944. Aircraft from 464 Squadron (RAAF) played an important part in the operations of 2 TAF. *(RAAF)*

target the loss should, statistically, have been one hundred times greater . . .

If these weapons had been fired at the assembly and despatch areas of our invasion forces there might have been no landing in Normandy. The war would then have dragged on for many months and might even have ended in an Allied defeat.

The Mosquito's contribution to the reduction of this threat is specially notable when compared with those of the American Fortress, Marauder, Boston and Mitchell aircraft, and the British Typhoon.

For example, while the large four-engined Fortress bombers destroyed 30 sites for an average of 195.1 tons of bombs per site, and with an average loss of 1.1 aircraft per site destroyed, the little wooden Mosquito put 19 sites out of action for a tonnage of 39.8 and a loss of 0.87 aircraft per site.[1] Moreover there were two men in each lost Mosquito, as against the Fortress which could field enough men to make a cricket eleven.

The New Zealanders of 487 Squadron, with 21 (British) and 464 (Australian), formed 140 Wing in the RAF's 2 Group. This Group belonged to the new Allied 2nd Tactical Air Force which, late in 1943,

---

[1] These figures are quoted from *Mission Completed* by Air Chief Marshal Sir Basil Embry, GCB, KBE, DSO, DFC, AFC (Methuen, 1957).

despite the desperate distraction of the flying bomb sites, began to prepare the way for the invasion of Normandy.

The Air Officer Commanding No. 2 Group was Basil Embry, now an Air Vice Marshal and more than ever enamoured of the Mosquito. He built up eight Mosquito squadrons in his Group, and they were, as it used to be said, well and truly 'Basilized'. The crews, inspired by Embry's leadership and love for the Mosquito — he flew 19 operational sorties with them as an Air Vice Marshal — brought new glory to the name of the little wooden aeroplane they all loved so well.

Embry's eight squadrons made a speciality of daylight low-level pinpoint attacks on houses and buildings known to contain Gestapo records and dossiers.

But first Embry had to put up a fight to get Mosquitos for his Group which, as he assumed command, was operating Bostons, Mitchells and Venturas.

The story is best told in the Air Chief Marshal's own words:[1]

> I was anxious that the number of aircraft types should be reduced to two, the Mitchell and the Mosquito VI, which seemed best suited to the role approved for the Group. The Boston was a good aeroplane

[1] Quoted from *Mission Completed*.

A Royal Australian Air Force Mosquito. *(RAAF, via Stuart Howe)*

A factory fresh FB.VI up on a test flight before joining its squadron. *(via Stuart Howe)*

but it was seventy miles an hour slower than the Mosquito VI, and carried only a third of the bomb load of the Mitchell. It was also in short supply, and as I had been warned that it would be impossible to maintain more than two squadrons of them over the next year, there was a strong argument that they should be superseded. I was relieved to learn that there was also a shortage of Venturas, because I was especially anxious that our four squadrons of these aircraft should be re-equipped as soon as possible, their performance falling far short of what was needed for operations over North-West Europe.

When I raised the matter with Headquarters 2nd Tactical Air Force, I learned that the Air Ministry had decided to re-equip the Group with the Vengeance, an American aeroplane we were getting in exchange for Mosquitos. I at once arranged to borrow one from the experimental unit at Boscombe Down to test its performance and was dismayed to find that it was below that of the Battle which had been unable to survive the conditions experienced in North-West Europe in 1940 . . .

Its rear armament was quite inadequate, consisting of one small-calibre gun which could not be depressed to fire below the horizontal, it was too slow to be escorted by Spitfires and so could not be used on day operations, and it was too sluggish and cumbersome to be used for ground strafing at night. In fact it was nothing but a menace.

I went straight to Leigh-Mallory armed with this information, who told me I was just in time as a conference was to take place at the Air Ministry within a few days to decide the equipment for the 2nd Tactical Air Force, and he invited me to accompany him.

The meeting was told that a decision had already been taken about the future aircraft for 2 Group, but Leigh-Mallory insisted that my views should be heard, and I expressed them politely but forcibly when I brought up the subject of the Vengeance. I was the only person in the room to have flown it and this was greatly to my advantage when I discussed its shortcomings. The outcome was highly satisfactory: six of our squadrons were re-equipped with Mosquito VI's[1] and the Vengeance was never used in the western theatre of war. If it had been, casualties would inevitably have been very high indeed. It proved impossible to reduce the number of aircraft types in the Group to two, and the two squadrons of Bostons were kept until the end of the war.

Embry having won the Mosquito for the majority of his squadrons, Hereward de Havilland was very soon on the Group's doorstep in that much-travelled flying club machine, his Leopard Moth.

In the autumn of 1943 he reported to his brother and to the company:

Including the Conversion Flight, there are about 75 Mosquitos at Sculthorpe and no other type. Pickard, the Station Commander, has a large country house as a Mess, and so far I have always had partridges for lunch there, and a hare to bring home.

On 2nd October, the Group carried out its first operation with Mosquitos, 24 of which, together with 36 Bostons, attacked two power stations north of St Nazaire, each Mosquito carrying four 500-lb. M.C.[2] bombs.

The first wave bombed from treetop height and the remainder from 800 feet. Both targets were well covered with direct hits, but several of the delayed action bombs bounced 400 yards. No fighters were seen but there was considerable flak over the targets. Embry himself flew on this trip, taking David Atcherley as navigator. The Mosquitos left from Exeter and all returned. Pickard landed at Predannock, having flown all the way back on one engine owing to a lump of flak in a radiator. Patterson, flying a Mark IV with ciné

[1] There were later a total of eight Mosquito squadrons in the Group.
[2] Medium-case.

camera in the nose, had most of the rear part of the cockpit roof blown off by a shell and four other aircraft, including Embry's, were damaged. Nobody was hurt. Four Bostons were lost.

The second Mosquito operation took place on 9th October and was a costly failure. Twenty-four aircraft of 464 and 487 Squadrons took off from Sculthorpe at 11.15 a.m. to bomb an aircraft plant near Metz. After crossing the English coast they ran into thick weather and about eight miles out had to go off course to miss a very large British convoy flying balloons, of which they had had no warning. Visibility decreased to 400 yards and the formations lost touch before reaching the French coast, where Squadron Leader Davey saw a flak battery winding their guns round like mad to bring them to bear, as they had luckily been pointing in the wrong direction (probably that of the previous wave).

In France, the clouds were right down on the hills and no aircraft reached the target.

Unknown to me, or I think anyone else outside Sculthorpe, the intercom switches of these aircraft had been altered to press-buttons on the control column, close to the bomb-release switch, and it is probable that this accounts for two of the four aircraft that were lost. All were flying at near sea-level, and one was seen to disintegrate with a colossal explosion just before, and another some time after, crossing the French coast. The explosions were consistent with the bursting of bombs with instantaneous fuses, released at this sort of height.

The second wave of aircraft carried instantaneous-fuse bombs only, and for this reason were unable to attack any targets they happened to see owing to the low level at which the weather forced them to fly. Some pilots carrying eleven-second delay bombs did have a go at factory buildings and canal barges.

I drove round with Pickard to each aircraft as they came in to Sculthorpe. Most crews had little idea where they had been to and all were roundly cursing the weather, the convoy, and instantaneous bombs. All windscreens were plastered thick with flies which didn't improve some of the landings. Four leading edges and two main spars were damaged by birds. Squadron Leader Wilson landed at Manston, his observer killed by flak.

There is little doubt, I think, that this operation would have been less costly had some of the old hands of 105 and 139 Squadrons been in charge of briefing and formations. The failure to report the presence of the convoy and the unsatisfactory met. information have been taken up strongly by the Group.

The 'old hands' — Nos. 105 and 139 Squadrons — who had so gloriously blazed the low-level daylight trail were now in Pathfinder

Model used for briefing before the Amiens prison raid.

Bennett's No. 8 Group. The crews of No. 2 Group, however, soon learned the trade which such wily and earlier birds as Channer, Oakeshott, Edwards and Wooldridge had introduced.

The Pickard who fed Major de Havilland on partridge and sent him home with a hare was the Station commander at Sculthorpe. Only 29 and a Group Captain, with three DSO's and a DFC, he was widely known as the anonymous star of the film *Target for Tonight* — as the pilot of 'F for Freddie'. He died in a Mosquito, together with his navigator Flight Lieutenant Broadley, DSO, DCM, DFM, while leading a Mosquito force in yet another role — as a prison buster.

Snow and sleet were falling over the sea when eighteen Mosquitos of Nos. 21, 464 and 487 Squadrons — No. 140 Wing — set off on 18th February 1944. It was filthy flying weather. Low clouds blanketed the route. The operation would have been called off had it not been for a last-moment, desperate appeal from the French underground. More than 100 people, collected from prisons all over France, were facing execution in Amiens prison.

In the words of the No. 140 Wing report, 'The operation was planned with the intention of breaking the walls of the prison to assist the escape of 120 French prisoners condemned to death for helping the Allies. In the event of failure they requested the whole of the building to be bombed.'

Operation Jericho, to give this raid its code name, had been planned for some time and a model of the prison had been made from reconnaissance photographs for the briefing of crews. To attack at low level and breach the prison walls — this was red meat for Mosquito pilots, and Air Vice Marshal Embry had decided to lead the Wing himself. But he was ordered not to do so.

Of this disappointment Embry has written: 'Charles Pickard led instead of me and I shall always regret that decision because, although he was an exceptionally experienced operational pilot at night, he had carried out only a few missions by day, and I believe this may well have been the reason he was shot down by enemy fighters.

The Mosquitos were to approach in three waves, but Pickard was to call off the attack at any moment that he considered his purpose achieved. As his crews pressed home their attack, Pickard orbited the prison. Two waves went in and from his 'grandstand' view he could see numbers of prisoners running out through the wall breaches.

Calculating that sufficient damage had been done and that additional bombing might cause unnecessary loss of life, the young Group Captain ordered the third wave to withdraw. But at that moment he saw one of

Group Captain P. C. Pickard, DSO, DFC, whose face was well known to the public as the captain of 'F for Freddie' in the film *Target for Tonight*. He died leading the Amiens raid.

91

Reconnaissance photographs taken after the raid. In the lower right-hand corner can be seen the breach through which the prisoners escaped.

Low-level picture of an attack on a target at The Hague.

his Mosquitos, piloted by Squadron Leader MacRitchie, fall to a hail of light flak, and decided to investigate.

It was then that, detached from the fighter escort covering the withdrawal of his three formations, this great airman was shot down — 'bounced' by a pair of Fw 190's.

The bodies of Pickard and Broadley, his navigator, after being recovered by friendly French villagers, were seized by the Germans and buried in a cemetery near the prison. But more than two hundred and fifty prisoners had escaped, though sadly many were quickly recaptured and at least a hundred had been killed by the bombs.

Neither Pickard nor his Mosquito has ever been forgotten by the French. Parts of the aircraft were picked up and hidden by French patriots. They lie embedded in a memorial at Amiens.

Before and after D-Day there were more daylight pinpoint attacks in the spirit of Amiens. Aimed at killing and confounding the Gestapo, they also succeeded in assisting the escape of prisoners and destroying evidence collected against resistance patriots.

Mosquito attack on Gestapo HQ at Aarhus. German staff cars can be seen parked in front of the building.

The first major raid of this description after Amiens took place on 11th April 1944. Wing Commander R. H. Bateson, C.O. of No. 613 Squadron, leading six Mosquitos, attacked a five-storey Gestapo building opposite the Peace Palace at The Hague. Two bombs entered by the front door.

The Mosquito was also a welcome visitor over the rooftops of Denmark — an out-of-season Father Christmas with some very explosive parcels for Gestapo chimneys. Air Vice Marshal Embry flew in No. 2 Group's low-level Denmark raids, which are now legendary. The first was to Aarhus on 31st October 1944, when eighteen Mosquitos of No. 140 Wing (now commanded by Wing Commander Wykeham-Barnes), singled out Gestapo offices in a building at Aarhus University. The attack was pressed home from a very low level, Squadron Leader F. H. Denton bringing home a piece of aged and learned masonry in his fuselage to prove it.

At Copenhagen the Gestapo had installed themselves in Shell House. As usual all briefing precautions were taken to avoid death and injury to the Danish people. In this case the pinpoint task was not quite as exacting as usual. One nearby building was used as a German brothel. It was not the target, but if a stray bomb hit it, well . . .

But in war the best laid plans will be upset by the unexpected. Wing Commander Kleboe, the C.O. of No. 21 Squadron, hit a bridge and crashed into a school. Unhappily, some of the following aircraft took this scene of smoke and destruction for the target and bombed it with their accustomed accuracy. Many little Danes died as the Mosquitos fulfilled their mission.[1] In the chaos at Shell House, some Gestapo officers were killed and all the prisoners escaped. The Mosquitos had bombed with an accuracy that secured this remarkable double dividend, in spite of the disastrous bombing of the school; and these raids gave a great lift to Danish morale when the German occupiers, and the strutting Gestapo, were now seen to be in fear of their lives themselves.

It is another tribute to the Mosquito's versatility and mechanical efficiency that these pinpoint raids were carried out by aircraft and crews primarily engaged on other work during the same period — the support of the invasion forces.

[1] On 17th August 1945, Air Chief Marshal Sir W. Sholto Douglas presented a cheque for 470,000 *kroner* (about £20,000) to the Crown Prince of Denmark at Aarhus. The cheque represented a contribution from the RAF to aid Danes injured in raids on Gestapo H.Q. at Aarhus, Copenhagen and Odense.

Chapter 11
The Berlin Express

'A clear, beautiful summer's day. Everyone who could, leaped into the air.' No. 25 Squadron might perhaps have been recording an aerial picnic on their Form 540. Indeed, the summer days of 1944 *were* beautiful as Mosquito crews swept over Normandy, shirt-sleeved and open-necked, over the bloody *bocage* below, where every soldier, his neck aching under a tin hat, looked thankfully upwards.

Mosquito crews flew day and night, some pilots and navigators making as many as three sorties in twenty-four hours. On 13th August seventy-nine pilots in No. 2 Group made two sorties each during the night.

RAF doctors recorded that the crews were standing up to the pressure, but cautioned that there was nevertheless a 'marked element of strain'. The doctors felt that, although no ill effects had resulted medically, it was questionable from the operational outlook whether crews were fresh enough, or sufficiently alert, to give full value. But the airmen could now see that the end of the war in Europe would reward their endeavours. The Mosquito aircraft supported the stamina of the crews with a mechanical constancy which was so uncanny as to appear sympathetic.

Aid from the air for the troops fighting their way into Normandy called for great accuracy in bombing. This, General Montgomery learned, was just the kind of air support which the Mosquito could give him.

On the afternoon of 30th July a formation of Mosquitos marked the ground for an attack by 250 heavy bombers in support of Montgomery's encircling movement around Caen. The Mosquitos rootled out and exposed a concentration of enemy tanks behind Monty's troops at a crossroads just west of Villers Bocage. The raid resulted in the devastation of a target area the size of the Arsenal football ground. Next day Monty signalled his especial thanks to the Royal Air Force.

A week later the General called in the Mosquitos again for a particularly accurate piece of 'X-marks-the-spot' bombing. British and Canadian troops had launched a strong attack but were meeting stiff opposition. They were only 2,000 yards from the bombers' target area. Once more the Mosquitos earned the General's thanks.

In those days, service pilots painted their aeroplanes with pet names. Wives, girlfriends, sweethearts, dogs, children, drinks — all found their way on to a Mosquito's nose. Most of the names were straightforward, since the airman who goes to war from a house called 'Ingle Nook' or 'Sea View' will name his aeroplane with about as much originality. But in No. 21 Squadron of Embry's No. 2 Group, in the summer of 1944, there appeared a Mosquito with a name which mystified everybody — except the 'driver'. For what possible reason, the air and ground crews wondered, did Flying Officer Freeman fly a Mossie named 'Folly'?

This twenty-one-year-old pilot had flown his first operational sortie with No. 21 Squadron five days before D-Day. He was Sir Wilfrid Freeman's son by the Air Chief Marshal's first marriage. The arrival of a Freeman flying a 'Folly' gave the Freeman family quite a vested interest in the welfare of the little wooden aeroplane.

Keith Freeman had been a schoolboy at Rugby when his father put through that first order for fifty Mosquitos. Now, as he flew a Mosquito operationally, the annual production figures were mounting. From 442 in 1942 built at the de Havilland, Hatfield and Leavesden factories to 1,185 in 1943, and 1,788 in 1944. At home two new main Mosquito contractors were also in full swing. Standard Motors built 42 Mosquitos in 1943 and 470 in 1944. Percival Aircraft built 49 in 1944. Airspeed at Christchurch, near Bournemouth — and today a subsidiary of de Havilland — were to come into production in 1945.

Overseas, Canada-built Mosquitos increased from 90 in 1943 to 419 in 1944. Australia began production in 1944 with 27 Mosquitos.[1]

Meanwhile the repair organization was providing an average of one in every four Mosquitos delivered for operations.

Delivery of Mosquitos to squadrons was undertaken by the golden-winged pilots of the Air Transport Auxiliary, serving under their banker Commodore, Gerard D'Erlanger. Many of the new aeroplanes were

---

[1] When the *very* last Mosquito had been wheeled out of the production hangar at the de Havilland Chester factory on 15th November 1950, the final figures were:

de Havilland —	3,299 at Hatfield
	1,627 at Leavesden
	1,134 at Toronto, Canada
	208 at Sydney, Australia
	81 at Chester
Standard Motors —	1,065 at Coventry
Percival Aircraft —	245 at Luton
Airspeed —	122 at Christchurch
Total	7,781

LEGEND

83. Tail Wheel (Marstrand)
84. Navigation Light
85. Stowage Picketing Eyes
86. Stowage U C Locking Cap
87. U C Retracted
88. U C Jack
89. 500 lb. Bomb
90. Aileron Trimming Tab

91. Universal Bomb Carrier (Wing)
92. Firewall
93. Fire Extinguisher Bottle Mk. II
94. Stub Exhausts
95. Broad Bladed Prop.
96. Spinner
97. Cockpit Canopy

98. Radio Remote Control Boxes
99. Pilot's Pouch
100. Pilot's Demand Regulator (Oxygen)
101. Dimmer Switches
102. Signal Cartridges
103. Fire Extinguisher
104. Thermos Bottles
105. Glycol Spray
106. Tail Drift Sight
107. Ladder Stowage
108. Radiator Flap
109. Landing Light
110. Wing Bond Fairing
111. Landing Wheel
112. Brake Hose

113. Mud Guard
114. U C Doors
115. Entrance Door
116. Camera Window
117. Centre Fuel Tank
118. Bomb Bay Doors
119. Bomb Carriers (Fuselage)
120. Bomb Winch
121. Bomb Bay Door Jack
122. Ration Container
123. Engine Covers, Sleeping Bags, etc.
124. Controls Locking-Stowage
125. Signal Strips
126. Emergency Tool Kit
127. Rear Entry Door

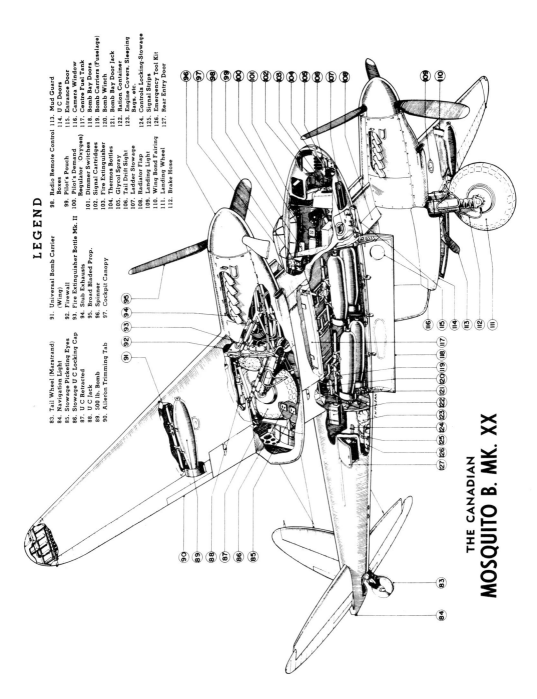

THE CANADIAN
MOSQUITO B. MK. XX

A cutaway view of a Canadian B.XX Mosquito. *(De Havilland of Canada Ltd, via Stuart Howe)*

FB.40s on the Bankstown assembly line. The aircraft in the foreground, A52-12, crashed on a pre-delivery test flight due to wing flutter at high speeds. A modification to the wing was then made to all Australian-built Mosquitos. *(via Stuart Howe)*

The cockpit of a B.XX on the Downsview, Ontario, assembly line, February 1944. *(Joe Holiday)*

flown to RAF bases by women ATA pilots, among them Lois Butler, the vivacious wife of Alan Butler, who was chairman of the de Havilland company when Mosquitos were being built.

Canadian Mosquitos presented a special delivery problem. How were these slender wooden aeroplanes to cross the Atlantic? To dismantle each aircraft, crate and ship it, would eat up time and freight space in addition to offering U-Boats several 'sitting pigeons' in one cargo. To hazard each Mosquito's chance across the gale-whipped Atlantic would speed up delivery, but at risk. Each new aeroplane would be in the hands of relatively inexperienced transatlantic fliers, making the crossing without adequate radio or navigational aids. In 1943-44 few pilots possessed a log-book of transatlantic 'hours'. There was no reserve of well-matured airline captains upon which to call.

But the ferry risks were accepted in face of operational demand for the Canada-built Mosquito. One by one, and sometimes in twos and threes, service pilots coaxed the new aeroplanes across an ocean that such men have called 'the Pond'.

There were losses. De Havilland, disturbed by the situation, sent Pat Fillingham, a 29-year-old test pilot, to fly a new Mosquito home and make a report. Fillingham's first attempt was abortive. Coming to Greenland for fuel, he met a blanket of fog and returned to Goose Bay. On a second attempt he made his first — and last — Atlantic flight in a Mosquito. He said afterwards that he hoped he would never be asked to repeat the experience.

To this day it is Fillingham's opinion that the principal reason for the losses was a bravado bred of inexperience among the men who disappeared and not the mechanical failure of the Mosquitos they flew.

The destruction of Germany proceeded as the land armies advanced. Mosquitos — British and Canadian-built — flew in the van of the air fleets which brought retribution down upon the heads of the nation that had believed it would never be bombed.

At the Ministry of Aircraft Production Sir Wilfrid Freeman had always insisted upon quality before quantity. It was this policy that made possible so many variations of the Mosquito's original theme of the unarmed speed bomber.

Towards the end of the war in Europe one of the many modifications developed behind the moat at Salisbury Hall enabled 'Bomber' Harris to send Mosquito formations over Germany in which each 'light bomber', with its crew of two, delivered as much high explosive as an eleven-man Flying Fortress — and with a very much greater chance of returning to bomb on another night.

This technical achievement stemmed from a day at Salisbury Hall when the de Havilland chief designer Bishop turned to his colleague

W. A. Tamblin, tape measure in hand, and said, 'Come on, Tam, how about putting the Mosquito in the family way?'

Off went the two designers to measure up a Mosquito's belly and to agree that they could 'just about do it'. The result was a very pregnant-looking aeroplane capable of dropping a 4,000-lb. bomb on Berlin — a variant of the Mosquito which at last brought the wooden aeroplane into full favour at the Air Ministry in its original 1938 concept as an unarmed speed bomber.

Minds were changed. Sir Edgar Ludlow-Hewitt, Inspector General of the Royal Air Force, now recommended the advantage of securing the maximum output of Mosquitos capable of carrying 4,000-lb. bombs.

'As the enemy's night defences improve,' he wrote to the Vice Chief of the Air Staff on 20th February 1944, 'the value of a very fast night bomber which can carry an effective load becomes more and more apparent.'

From the Ministry of Aircraft Production Freeman's staff had long since put forward a paper to the Air Ministry anticipating how

A pleasing view of B.XVI ML963 of 571 Squadron. ML963 was one of two Mosquitos that flew the Squadron's first operational sortie, and it also took part in the largest Mosquito raid on Berlin on 21st/22nd March 1945. *(via Stuart Howe)*

A Czech Air Force FB.VI. Because of a shortage of ammunition some of the guns on these Mosquitos were changed for German weapons, and the type was given the designation LB-36. *(John Stride)*

favourably, bombs dropped for targets hit for aircraft lost for man-hours spent, the fast little Mosquito would compare with the lumbering Lancaster, once it was carrying a 4,000-lb. bomb.

The suggestions in the MAP paper are interesting in the knowledge of Captain de Havilland's peacetime vision of large numbers of fast bombers to swamp enemy defences, although he had not in fact envisaged the possibility of his light aeroplane carrying such a load.

The paper pointed out that the Lancaster cost 2.8 times as much as the Mosquito in terms of standard man-hours, and maintenance was much in the same proportion. The Lancaster's average bomb load was 7,450 lb. (January to July 1943). The Mosquito with a 4,000-lb. bomb would average a 3,735-lb. load, allowing for abortive sorties. But whereas the Lancaster had averaged 28 sorties per write-off on night raids, the Mosquito's write-off average for night attacks was 92.

This meant, the paper explained, that the Mosquito could drop over four and a half times the weight of bombs for the same investment in Lancasters.

Thereafter, a Light Night Striking Force of Mosquito aircraft was built up. This Force attacked Germany relentlessly with formations of up to.50 Mosquitos on a night. It raided Berlin 170 times, maintaining one reign of terror over the enemy capital for 36 nights running.

The Mosquito arrivals became so routine that the Germans named the operation 'The Berlin Express'. The routes flown were 'Platforms 1, 2 and 3'.

101

Chapter 12
The Mosquito Goes to Sea

There was something different about the two Mosquitos which took off from the Coastal Command station at Predannock in Cornwall to look for U-Boats in the Bay of Biscay on the cold bleak morning of 4th November 1943.

Out of the nose of each aircraft protruded a heavy-looking tubular object which, from a distance, might have been taken for a piece of piping. It was, in the careful nomenclature of security, a 'Special Weapon'. The crews of the Mosquitos were on detachment to No. 248 Squadron from No. 618, that most secret of RAF Mosquito squadrons which was later to sail for the Pacific with the Royal Navy.

Formation of Australian Mosquitos from 464 Squadron RAAF setting out to attack enemy lines of communication behind the battle line in Normandy 1944. *(via Stuart Howe)*

PF606, which was built as a B.XVI and converted to TT.39 by General Aircraft Ltd of Feltham. *(via Stuart Howe)*

The pilots, Squadron Leader Rose, commanding the No. 618 detachment, and Flying Officer D. J. Turner, a peacetime Police Constable from the Romford Division at Hornchurch, were setting out to search in company along the French coast of the Bay of Biscay for homing U-Boats. They saw none. But chancing upon several fishing smacks with an armed trawler close by, they decided to try the 'Special Weapon' for the first time in action.

The Mosquitos dived to attack. Hits were scored and there was an explosion in the trawler's boilers, just before Rose's aircraft was hit by the ship's gunners. It began to smoke, crashed into the sea and disintegrated. Squadron Leader Rose and his navigator, Flight Sergeant S. Cowley, were lost, but they had proved the effectiveness of the 'Special Weapon' against shipping.

Thus, gallantly if tragically, had started the career of the 'Tsetse' edition of the Mosquito as a ship- and submarine-buster. The 'Special Weapon' was a quick-firing six-pounder — a flying field gun.

Coastal Command's employment of a light aeroplane, which combined fighter manoeuvrability and the punch of a field gun with the momentum of a dive attack, came as a shock to enemy submarine commanders and skippers of light shipping. It was a most unwelcome surprise, which owed much to the ingenuity and enterprise of Desmond Molins, who in peacetime was a manufacturer of cigarette-making machinery. He developed the ammunition feed which made it possible to protrude such a large and heavy weapon from the nose of so light and small an aeroplane.

U-Boats nearing their bases after a long and tiring patrol slunk towards port in fear of this new menace, and the enemy was obliged to find ship and fighter escorts for his homing submarines.

Landing a Mark TR.33 Mosquito on the deck of an aircraft carrier.

The first Tsetse attack on a U-Boat was made by two Mosquitos patrolling south of Brest. Flying Officer A. L. Bonnett of the RCAF and Flying Officer D. J. Turner were flying at 800 feet and just below cloud base when they spotted a submarine six miles away on the port beam. The U-Boat had seen them and was zig-zagging violently.

Bonnett dived into a hail of the U-Boat's flak. He fired one round, and then to his horror the six-pounder seized with a gun stoppage. Cursing his luck the Canadian pilot continued to make dummy attacks in order to draw some of the fire from Turner, who, making three attacks of six shells apiece, scored several hits before the submarine crash-dived with such alacrity that one unfortunate German sailor was left in the water.

Despite direct hits from the six-pounder, the U-Boat was only damaged, for the low cloud had prevented the Mosquitos from diving at an angle steep enough to ensure penetration of the hull.

Soon afterwards four Mosquitos on patrol off Ushant were able to so damage a U-Boat that a Liberator, arriving on the scene, finished it off with depth charges.

The larger aircraft of Coastal Command did not, incidentally, hold a monopoly as depth-charge droppers. Another light little maritime version of the Mosquito was modified for this heavy work, and shortly after D-Day a Mosquito of No. 333 Squadron — a Norwegian squadron operating Catalinas in 'A' Flight and Mosquitos in 'B' Flight — depth-charged a U-Boat from a height of only 30 feet. The depth charge hit the deck, bounced off, and exploded alongside the submarine's bow. The starboard bows shot up into the air and the U-Boat slewed round. Then it dropped beneath the waves.

The Tsetse and depth-charge Mosquito crews were keen U-Boat hunters, and they attended an anti-U-Boat school run by the Navy at Ballykelly to put themselves on top line for the task. The comprehensive course covered anti-submarine warfare from the earliest days to the latest tactics.

In the classroom, somewhat to their astonishment, they were told that during the 1914-18 war a pet seal had been taken to sea, kept on a starvation diet, and put overboard in waters believed to be submarine-infested. The theory was that the seal would find the refuse released by U-Boats.

They also heard that there had been a scheme to draft a cowboy to each submarine chaser. Recruited from the Wild West and put into naval uniform, he was supposed to lasso the periscope so that a bomb might be threaded on to the rope and slid down into the enemy conning tower! Alas, there is no evidence to show that seals or cowboys subsequently flew on operational service with the Mosquito crews of Coastal Command.

Towards the end of the war in Europe, Coastal Command's Mosquito squadrons were sweeping the sea for U-Boats, enemy convoys, escort vessels and minesweepers. On and around D-day their job was to prevent U-Boats and other craft from reaching the invasion forces, and to stop enemy submarines from breaking out of the Bay of Biscay and the Channel Ports.

While the Light Night Striking Force of Mosquito bombers flew night after night over Germany in its twenties, thirties, forties and fifties, a new Sea Strike Force was building up under the station command of

A Mosquito making an attack on a U-Boat.

A fine shot of Standard Motors-built FB.VI HR632 which joined 248 Squadron of Coastal Command in January 1945 at Banff in Scotland. The squadron used their Mosquitos on anti-shipping strikes along the Norwegian coast. Along with their nose mounted cannon and machine guns, these Mosquitos were invariably equipped with eight 60-lb rockets which were highly effective against shipping. HR632 was lost in action on 13th March 1945. *(Charles E. Brown)*

Group Captain the Hon. Max Aitken, Battle of Britain fighter ace and son of the proprietor of the *Daily Express* who had been Minister of Aircraft Production in those darker days when 'Freeman's Folly' stood in jeopardy of Ministerial displeasure. Group Captain Aitken was Station Commander at Banff. His Mosquito force, known as the Banff Strike Wing, comprised several Coastal Command squadrons in which the Mosquito had gradually replaced the redoubtable, but slower and more vulnerable Beaufighter.

Mosquitos of the Banff Strike Wing quickly established a reputation for their daring in low-level attack, much in the tradition of the Nos. 105 and 139 Squadron pioneers. And, if there were no chimney pots or telegraph wires to bring back as proof of the audacity of their attacks, there was always a ship's pennant.

Four days before V.E. Day, when 48 Mosquitos led by Wing Commander Foxley-Norris were sweeping the Kattegat, Flight Lieutenant G. N. E. Yeates with his navigator, Flight Lieutenant T. C. Scott, of No. 248 Squadron carried away a spar and pennant from the masthead of an enemy destroyer. When the Mosquito landed at base, the German pennant was fluttering from the Mosquito's nose.

Inshore, too, great things were done by a mine-laying Mosquito, which, skimming low over the canals in daylight, plopped her load in the path of enemy barge traffic. The fast and manoeuvrable Mossie might have been tailor-made for this dangerous job. Canal zones were among the most heavily defended parts of the Reich. While some Mosquitos were laying mines, others, flying low along the flak-bristling canal banks, purposely drew the fire of the concentrated ground defences. Ace pilots at baiting the flak gunners into action were Wing Commander F. F. Lambert, Squadron Leader H. B. Martin and Flight Lieutenant W. R. Butterfield of No. 515 Squadron, whose crews dauntlessly presented themselves as targets along the Kiel, Dortmund-Ems and Kaiser Wilhelm canals.

Over land and over sea some of the fast unarmed photographic-reconnaissance Mosquitos had meanwhile spread their wooden wings across the world as courier aircraft, their pilots the global errand-boys of Whitehall. Brass hats, diplomats, politicians and civil servants discovered that the range and speed of this aircraft enabled them to pass their paper around the place with such unprecedented promptitude that sometimes a Mosquito would touch down at its destination before the reception of the signal announcing its departure.

One courier pilot of No. 544 Squadron, already distinguished for his photographic reconnaissance of the *Tirpitz*, was Squadron Leader F. L. Dodd. He and his navigator, sports writer Eric Hill, flew the first diplomatic bag to Moscow for Mr Churchill's autumn meeting with Stalin in 1944.

The first of eleven round trips to Moscow by Mosquito crews of No. 544 Squadron between the 8th and 23rd of October, Dodd's flight was eventful, but not over the eastern war front, where he had expected trouble. His main problem was to match the information on the RAF's maps of Russia with the terrain below. The maps were out of date and on a very small scale. Dodd and Hill had expected to read their way to Moscow, like club fliers, with the help of the railway lines. To their dismay the lines on the map were no longer there on the ground. The Russians had moved them.

Then, as pilot and navigator were trying to sort out which town was which, a formation of Russian fighters appeared, gave chase, and opened fire with tracer. Fortunately the fire was inaccurate and Dodd decided that the Russian pilots must either be very bad shots, or 'letting off' in a burst of comradely high spirits. Nevertheless, taking no chances, he opened up to 330 m.p.h. and left the fighters comfortably behind.

Once Dodd and his sky-blue Mark XVI Mosquito were on the ground the Russians could not do enough for crew and machine. For the men there was VIP treatment: vodka, caviare, seats at the Bolshoi Theatre; for the aeroplane, reverential regard. A glyco leak had developed and the Mosquito was serviced tenderly by a little man in a cloth cap who astonished Dodd with his detailed engineering knowledge of the type.

Throughout 'Operation Frugal', as the courier service to the Moscow conference was known, there prevailed a spirit of warm comradeship between the Mosquito crews and Russian officers. Vodka flowed and the British crews were given bottles to take home. Upon their return to base,

A Sea Mosquito TR.33. *(via Stuart Howe)*

after pilots and navigators had removed their liquid perks, the servicing crews found comradely tidings scrawled in English to 'the brave British ground crews'.

But, alas, no vodka.

Celebration was a centre-piece of life in Mosquito squadrons. The cavalier cameraderie among the crews matched the rakish character of their aeroplane. There were gargantuan parties, for some of which pilots were despatched to round up the drink. One Mosquito, flying a 'hooch' sortie to Naples from Malta, returned with 60 bottles.

No. 100 Group, which included the Mosquito bomber support squadrons, marked the Group's 100th victim at a great party, and Wing Commander N. B. R. Bromley, commanding No. 169 Squadron, was presented with a fine tankard in recognition of his Squadron's action in putting the hundred up.

Drinks downed were totted up as conscientiously as Huns bagged. On a free night after a period of operations, No. 21 Squadron helped to lower 890 pints. Sometimes fancy dress was worn. Geoffrey de Havilland flew by Mosquito to a Farnborough party — rigged as a tramp.

At a No. 85 Squadron dance Lieutenant Colonel Albert Stern, a nearby squire, presented the C.O., Wing Commander John Cunningham, with a Victory Cup. Individual victories were inscribed on it.

One day before victory against Germany the last Mosquito to be lost in action in Europe made a crash landing. It was Mosquito M.V.530, and it fell from the skies over Germany — to American guns.

Finally, Mosquitos marked the areas for Lancasters dropping food to

DK296 left for Russia on 20th April 1944 — the Russians were interested in building the Mosquito under license. The aircraft saw operational service with 105 Squadron and flew 15 sorties. *(via Stuart Howe)*

the population of Holland — an operation called 'Manna', which No. 105 Squadron recorded as 'work worthy of our accuracy'.

And then a series of 'Cook's Tours' set in — organized aerial visits to the bombed cities of Germany.

No. 21 Squadron kept a Diary. On V.E. Day these words were entered: 'The aircraft are idle like unwanted, penniless old friends, standing by the roadside begging coppers. Even the tender hands of the ground crews have forsaken them. Men who "drove" and those who found paths through the blackest night forget their once trusted craft.'

The Mossie's war in Europe was over. Next day No. 21 Squadron played cricket against the Australians of No. 464 Squadron — on a Belgian wicket.

Beyond any possible doubt or contradiction the Mosquito — the only British-built, fully operational aeroplane to have been designed and produced within the date-boundaries of the 1939-45 hostilities — was now recognized as the most versatile military aircraft of all time.

And yet, as the aircraft had almost served its purpose in Europe, it was obsolescent. At one and the same time as Berlin lay at the mercy of the Mosquito, London tautly awaited each sickening thump that announced the arrival of another Rocket, while, over Germany, the fading Luftwaffe's small numbers of jet and rocket fighters, the Me 262's and 163's, were more than a match for a piston-engined Mosquito.

But east of Calcutta, where men still fought, and also at sea, the Mosquito yet reigned supreme.

Chapter 13
East of Suez

On 17th October 1944, the aircraft carriers *Fencer* and *Striker* lay in the King George V dock at Glasgow. The 'buzz' on the mess decks said, 'We're going foreign.' The 'buzz' — this time — was correct. The aircraft carriers were preparing to join the new British Pacific Fleet.[1]

It was the forenoon. Shortly, aboard each carrier the bosuns' mates would pipe 'Up Spirits', some wag would murmur 'Stand fast the Holy Ghost', and all men not 'Under Age' or 'Temperence' would draw their grog.

But first some most unseamanlike happenings were to take place. A party of 'light blue jobs' was observed mounting the gangway. And there, on the flight deck after being hoisted inboard, stood a Mosquito.

To their astonishment the man of *Striker* and *Fencer* learned that they were embarking a number of these twin-engine land bombers — complete with RAF crews.

At last, and towards the end of its operational career, the Mosquito upon which the Navy had once had such strong designs as a target tower, was going to sea in squadron service — manned by the RAF. On the last day of October 1944, No. 618 Squadron of the Royal Air Force sailed with the Royal Navy to the Pacific. Their mission was to attack the Japanese Fleet with the dam-buster type of spinning spherical bombs.

Although the RAF crews had carried out exercises with the escort carrier *Rajah* in single-engine Fleet Air Arm Barracuda torpedo-bombers, they were without deck landing and take-off experience in a twin-engined Mosquito. Taking off and landing a Mosquito on a carrier flight deck had, however, been proved possible during intrepid experiments

---

[1] The Fleet began its formal existence on 22nd November 1944, when Admiral Fraser hoisted his flag as Commander-in-Chief, first in the gunboat *Tarantula* and later in the battleship *Howe*.

An RAF reconnaissance Mosquito flying over the summit of Mount Everest.

carried out several months earlier by Lieutenant-Commander E. M. Brown of the Fleet Air Arm.[1]

The carriers arrived at Melbourne in time for Christmas, but events marched ahead of them. By June 1945, their prospects of operations had faded away. The Mosquitos joined the Royal Australian Air Force. Ground crews lent a hand on Australian airfields while they awaited repatriation. Air crews were posted off to India.

Although the Mosquito's guest months with the Navy had come to nought, the experience was not wasted. It opened the seaborne hangar doors to yet another edition of the wooden aeroplane — D.H. designer W. A. Tamblin's Sea Mosquito with folding wings for carrier stowage and a new, if short-lived, role as a naval torpedo-bomber.[2]

Flying Mosquitos from airfields in India and strips in Burma, the RAF presented a photographic survey to the map-makers of the Fourteenth Army.

Far from the climatically cooler, if militarily warmer, skies of Europe,

[1] On 25th March 1944, Lieutenant-Commander E. M. Brown, MBE, DSC, Chief Naval Test Pilot at the Royal Aircraft Establishment, landed Mosquito L.R.359, a Mark 6 fighter-bomber, on the deck of HMS *Indefatigable* off the west coast of Scotland. This was the first time that a twin-engined aeroplane had ever been landed on a ship at sea. The Mosquito had an arrester hook fitted to a strengthened fuselage. Seven successful landings were made.

[2] Mr Tamblin's brilliant 'navalizing' of the Mosquito — especially the provision of folding wings — introduced a new era of naval aircraft building for the de Havilland company. There followed the Sea Hornet, Sea Vampire, Sea Venom and Sea Vixen — all developed under Mr Tamblin's direction at Christchurch near Bournemouth.

the versatile Mosquito once more employed its probing combination of range and speed for reconnaissance. The results obtained were beyond the utmost capacities of the Buffaloes, Blenheims, even the Hurricanes and Spitfires in first-line service over the jungles of South-East Asia.

The Mosquito was far in advance of any light aircraft yet operated against the Japanese. Its arrival in India for weathering trials in 1943 caused a sensation. Squadrons that were asked merely to sample the first six aircraft flown out from home pressed them into operational service. And there were mishaps. Major de Havilland, following the Mosquito east of Suez — but not, need it be said, in his faithful Leopard Moth — was horrified to find Mosquitos 'coming unstuck' and miniature gardens of fungus taking root along their wooden wings and fuselages. He experienced great opposition when he tried to persuade the eager pilots not to fly until each machine had been inspected and passed as serviceable. On one occasion the Major was obliged to resort to a desperate measure in order to demonstrate that he really meant what he said. He bought a hacksaw, knelt on a Mosquito's wing and solemnly worked his way through it in the heat of the midday sun!

The glue troubles were overcome and, after a number of tragic disintegrations, Mosquitos made a major contribution to the defeat of the Japanese in Burma, No. 684 Squadron photographing 232,100 square miles for the Army in 3,000 flying hours between November 1943 and May 1944.

In terms of mechanical efficiency and human stamina the record of the

Burma, 1945. FB.VI of 82 Squadron flown by Vic Hewes attacking Japanese positions.
(Stuart Howe)

Mosquito and its crews in South-East Asia is remarkable. Reconnaissance requirements called for long flights of five, six, seven and sometimes eight or nine hours over jungle and sea for the two men in each cockpit — one pilot and one navigator.

Fighter and flak hazards were negligible by European experience, but machines and crews faced opposition from factors which appeared all the more fearsome for their very inhumanity: the climate, the monsoon, the terrain and the knowledge of the torture that could be expected in Japanese hands. And down there, as a reminder of Japanese treatment of their prisoners, lay the Burma-Siam death railway. Mosquito crews knew it well. They photographed it milestone by milestone.

Month by month as the 'recce' crews extended their range, the prospective 'walk home' became longer and longer, until No. 684 Squadron's Mosquitos were covering all Burma, half Indo-China and much of Thailand.

These Mosquitos flew round trips of 1,860 miles to Bangkok, 2,172 to the Malay Peninsula, 2,341 to cover Moulmein and the Bangkok-Phnom Penh railway, 2,493 to cover the Bangkok-Singapore railway to a point south of the Malayan frontier. There was one marathon sortie of 2,620 miles from the Cocos Islands to photograph Penang and Taiping, which took more than nine hours to complete. From all No. 684 Squadron's reconnaisance sorties between December 1943 and April 1945, only three Mosquitos were missing.

Range was almost an obsession for South-East Asia reconnaissance. Every possible ruse was employed to extend it. One tactic, as the Fourteenth Army moved forward in Burma, was to fly up to a strip and refuel a few miles from the Japanese. On such occasions pilot and navigator would carry an overnight bag in the cockpit. That night they slept, revolvers buckled round their pyjama trousers — yes, they took pyjamas to the front for a good night's sleep in a *basha*. Then at dawn they would take off for the long and lonely flight over the endless carpet of green. That night in the *basha* had given them some precious new mileage.

No. 684 Squadron also flew some very long sorties over the sea. Flying Officer J. J. Bannister and Warrant Officer C. G. Hoppitt were returning from a trip over the Nicobar Islands on 25th January 1945, when a most disconcerting thing happened. High over the Bay of Bengal, Hoppitt, turning to look at his companion, noticed to his amazement that Bannister had begun to swell, and swell, and swell. Snap went the pilot's cockpit harness. Pop went his parachute straps. Ballooning larger and larger, Flying Officer Bannister was floating in the cockpit. As he ballooned even bigger his head became jammed up against the cockpit roof. Then his enormous 'stomach' forced the stick forward against the instrument panel — and the Mosquito pitched into a terrifyingly steep nose-dive. Just in time to save the aircraft from disaster the navigator pricked the ballooning pilot with his pencil. The pilot's rubber dinghy had decided to inflate itself.

While photo-recce Mosquitos were the eyes of the Army, bomber Mosquitos supported the soldiers as they pushed the Japanese back into Burma from the frontiers of India. Structural failures there were, but these did not deter the crews and there was much annoyance when aircraft were grounded. Wing Commander R. J. Walker, commanding No. 45 Squadron which had been operating Vengeance aircraft, commented in the Operations Record Book: 'The proved structural failures in the Mosquitos in this squadron do not seem to have affected the morale of the aircrews in any way and they are most enthusiastic about the aircraft . . . A firm hand is needed sometimes to stop some of the crews from pinching too many trips.'

Enthusiasm over the arrival of a squadron's Mosquitos equalled that shown at home. 'The greatest event for some time was the arrival of our Mosquitos. They were stared at with awe and reverence, so long have we waited,' No. 89 Squadron chronicled on 20th February 1945.

The same enthusiasm for the aeroplane, but a very different war for the crews. No tall, smoking industrial chimneys to bring home in a navigator's lap. No broad expanse of corrugated factory roof to aim for. In Burma the targets were Japanese field-gun positions, sampans ferrying men and ammunition along muddy, jungle-fringed streams, bullock carts camouflaged with green palm leaves. These were primitive conditions of warfare in comparison with Europe where the jet and the rocket had now outmoded the Mosquito.

When it was all over and the atom bomb had brought the war against the Japanese to a sudden close there was a feeling among Mosquito crews of incompletion. Wing Commander M. H. Constable-Maxwell, commanding No. 84 Squadron, expressed it when he entered these words into his Form 540 on V.J. Day:

'Feelings were mixed . . . The natural joy of peace again was tempered by the feeling that Japan was still unconquered and that the armies in Malaya and Japan were still victorious and would feel, like Germany in 1918, let down by their home front. Many aircrew, in addition, felt thwarted of their much longed-for "crack at the Jap".'

Despite this sense of disappointment, the Mosquito had made a notable contribution to the turn of the tide in South-East Asia before the Japanese surrender.

Finally, shortly before and not long after the end, Mosquito aircraft took part in three separate flights well in character with the aeroplane's colourful past.

As Rangoon fell, a Mosquito pilot, Wing Commander A. F. Saunders, seeing an area free from bomb craters at Mingaladon airfield, landed and was 'first in' to the capital of Burma. In the Wing Commander's words he 'appropriated a small sampan and proceeded down the Rangoon River

Four FB.VI's of 45 Squadron flying near St Thomas Mount, Madras, in India, December 1945. RF778 and RF953 nearest the camera. *(S. J. Findley via R. Bonser)*

NF.IX TA230 was built early in 1945 and was delivered to Pershore where it was made ready for its ferry flight to SEAC, arriving in Burma, 7th April 1945, where it was photographed and was SOC on 30th May 1946. *(T. Wildgoose, via Stuart Howe)*

on the ebb tide to tell the Navy the good news that the Japs had gone'. This he knew from his own observation and from a message painted on the roof of Rangoon Jail by prisoners: 'Japs gone — extract digit'.

A Mosquito was also early on the scene in Malaya, landing in Singapore a day ahead of re-occupation forces. The pilot, Flight Lieutenant C. G. Andrews, was a New Zealand member of No. 684 Squadron, who a few weeks earlier had flown a Mosquito over the top of Everest. Andrews, obliged to force-land on a photographic reconnaisance over the island, visited Changi Jail. To service his Mosquito he borrowed an engineer officer, a fitter and a rigger who had been prisoners for three and a half years. The Japs, now all teeth and courtesy, knew that within hours they would be the prisoners.

After the surrender Mosquitos were ordered to Malaya. This posed a problem for No. 89 Squadron, which possessed a bear called Vicky, for wherever the Squadron went, Vicky went too.

Vicky, so named because of a distinctive white V on her chest, had been bought as a cub in a Calcutta bazaar by squadron armourers out on a spree. When the squadron moved from Baigachi to Singapore, three unserviceable Mosquitos, their crews, and the bear were all that remained of the unit. The crew of one of the Mosquitos, Flying Officer Peter Varley and Warrant Officer Ken Lloyd decided to smuggle Vicky back to the Squadron.

Pilot, navigator and bear squeezed into the cockpit. After an air test in a repaired Mosquito, the two men and the bear set course for Rangoon. After a day or two there they flew to Singapore with a refuelling stop at Kuala Lumpur.

Here the bear was tethered to an undercarriage leg while the crew helped to 'fill up' with five-gallon cans. Unhappily, some petrol spilled over Vicky, who got very angry and when Lloyd tried to soothe her she bit him on the arm.

However, refuelling was hastened and the three occupants of the Mosquito hurried down to Singapore to get Lloyd to a doctor for an anti-bear injection.

At Singapore that evening, as daylight faded, a group of rather senior officers, who had not yet touched a 'sundowner', watched the Mosquito taxi up from the airfield.

What they said when the door of the cockpit opened and a large black bear jumped out has not been recorded.

Chapter 14
Mission Completed

When I set out to write this story, only three Mosquitos survived in regular RAF service in Britain. They were stationed at White Waltham near Maidenhead where, somewhat incongruously, they shared a grass airfield with Fairey Aviation's Rotodyne.

I spent several very pleasant days flying alongside Flight Lieutenant 'Digger' Webster, DFC, now in his forties, and a veteran of those stirring days I have been describing.

Our first trip was to Exeter where Webster was to examine a number of civilian pilots flying Mosquitos for a private firm under contract to tow targets for service gunners.

One of the pilots, 'Bam' Beaumont, had commanded a Mosquito

PR.34a RG314 was delivered to Benson in December 1945, and in 1950 it spent some time with de Havilland to overcome rogue characteristics. In March 1955 it was delivered to 81 Squadron at Tengah, where it plotted terrorist movements over the jungles of Malaya. On 15th December 1955 RG314 made the last operational flight of a Mosquito and it was SOC on 29th February 1956. *(via Chris Foulds)*

NF.XXX MM748 did not see Squadron service but was delivered to the A&AEE at Boscombe Down on 20th July 1944. After a period in store it was scrapped in November 1946. By the end of the war some 17 units had received NF.XXXs. *(via Stuart Howe)*

squadron at Exeter during the war. As a civilian he was still there — and still flying Mossies.

Our next visit was to Waddington where Wing Commander Frank Dodd, who had made that memorable flight to Moscow for Mr Churchill, proudly showed me just one of his V Force Vulcans.

At Waddington the welcome for the Mosquito was one of service-restrained rapture. The Station Commander, Group Captain S. L. Ring, drove out to greet us and remained on the apron to climb into the cockpit of the type which had brought him safely home from many photographic-reconnaissance sorties.

Young officers, jet-trained and strangers to piston-engined aircraft, joined groups of ground crew, who after watching us land as if we had arrived from outer space, gathered in curiosity to inspect this vintage wonder.

From Waddington we flew to Wittering, which had been an early base for the first Mosquito night fighters. There, Wing Commander Ivor Broom asked Webster's permission to sit in the Mosquito's cockpit. Broom, a Baptist Minister's son, of whom it was said during the war that 'he could drop a bomb on a postage stamp', had attacked Berlin many times as a Mosquito pilot.

In the office from which he commanded a magnificent view of his squadron of Valiant bombers, Broom — DSO, DFC and two bars, AFC — who was also a top tunnel-buster, thumbed through the pages of his log-book.

118

B.25 NI203V, ex-KA997, was bought by Dianna Bixby for an around-the-world record attempt which started on 2nd April 1950, but after take-off from Calcutta in India she had to return with a bad engine and the attempt was cancelled. The aircraft was then sold to the Flying Tiger Line who replaced the wooden cockpit with a metal one for high altitude photography. The aircraft was lost in a crash in January 1956. *(R. T. O'Dell)*

'Look at this,' he said. 'Berlin and back in under four hours. Not bad going — even now. Doesn't that surprise you?'

No. The Mosquito surprised the world.

On the second day of October 1958, twenty years after Munich, I stood in the garden of Salisbury Hall with John Cunningham. We talked of the Mosquito — and of the martins fluttering round the seventeenth-century chimneys, birds which would soon start their long journey to warmer climes.

Mr Cunningham had just flown the Comet 4 home from Hong Kong — in a day. We should really have been discussing the Comet, and as if to remind us of our defection, Pat Fillingham passed low overhead on his way to deliver the third of BOAC's Comet 4 Fleet at London Airport.

For some minutes John Cunningham and I watched the Goldsmiths' tabby cat playing with Bella, their black Labrador puppy. Then Sir Geoffrey de Havilland arrived, driving his Morris Minor across the moat. He apologized that he had been detained by a television interview about the new Comet.

We all went indoors. Past the kitchen where the telephone girl had fallen in love with the engineer; where in 1940 'Mrs Led', the Chief Designer's secretary, had supervised rock salmon for lunch — 'So good for the brain', as she would say. And into the room where Bishop had first pencilled the graceful lines of the Mosquito.

119

We were met as a Committee[1] to administer the Mosquito Appeal Fund which had been set up to raise money for the purchase and equipment of a hangar-museum in which W.4050, the very first Mosquito, could be visited by the public on the site of the cabbage patch where this same aeroplane had been born.

Mr Rendell reported that the fund had already collected £200 — 'or to be more precise', he said in Bank Manager language, 'the total will have reached that nice round figure once the dollar remittances have been cleared.'

'Dollars?' — 'D.H.' peered enquiringly over his spectacles. Yes, Mr Rendell told us, American and Canadian pilots who had flown the Mosquito during the war were rallying to the cause.

Oliver Goldsmith said we needed a total of £1,000 to complete the hangar purchase and asked if we felt we should proceed in the hope that the fund would build up.

There was a silence.

Many of the men associated with the first Mosquito had gone — John de Havilland, D.H.'s second son, killed in a wartime Mosquito-to-Mosquito collision over the home airfield of Hatfield with test pilot, George Gibbins; Geoffrey Raoul de Havilland, OBE, airman from his schooldays when in 1925 he flew a Moth home for the holidays from a Stowe playing-field with his father as instructor.[2] Sir Wilfrid Freeman, who worked himself to death.

'D.H.' looked over his glasses. 'We'll do it anyway,' he said. Four words from the heart. They had started the Mosquito's story. Now they were to end it.

More than 20 years have gone by and Sir Geoffrey de Havilland has been laid to rest since making the decision to bring the prototype Mosquito home to Salisbury Hall. At the time it could not be foreseen that W.4050 — still the centrepiece of the collection — would be joined by such a variety of historic de Havilland aircraft, engines and memorabilia that the lawns of Salisbury Hall were to become known as The Garden That Grows Aeroplanes. Nor could it be foreseen that so much hangar space would be required that the Mosquito Appeal Fund would raise many thousands of pounds, make regular contributions to The Royal Air Force Benevolent Fund and maintain its charitable status as the more recently formed de Havilland Museum Trust Limited.

[1] Committee of the Mosquito Appeal Fund: Mr W. J. 'Oliver' Goldsmith, Chairman, Sir Geoffrey de Havilland, Mr John Cunningham, Mr R. Rendell (Treasurer), Miss Constance Babington-Smith, Mr Charles Gibbs-Smith and the author.

[2] Chief Test Pilot of the de Havilland Aircraft Company, he died in the DH108 experimental jet aircraft on the eve of attempting to break the world record. In the fortnight before the accident Geoffrey de Havilland had attained time level speeds in excess of the then world record of 616 m.p.h.

Epilogue

It seems only yesterday that I first visited Salisbury Hall in 1958 and discovered how the prototype de Havilland Mosquito was designed and built there. As a result *The Wooden Wonder* was published in 1959 and has been reissued since in a series of editions.

Earlier this year (2000) and more than 40 years on I returned to Salisbury Hall to renew acquaintance with W 4050 and delight in the ever expanding collection of de Havilland aircraft, engines, memorabilia and bits and pieces which accompany the prototype.

However, it was reassuring to note that in one essential and emotive respect the scene had not changed since the day in 1959 when, as a founder member of the fundraising committee I attended the opening of the Mosquito Memorial Museum which still houses W 4050 as its priceless centrepiece.

I remembered a lunch in 1958 at which, after obtaining Sir Geoffrey de Havilland's blessing on my proposal to write this book, I suggested hesitantly that the pioneer aviator and aircraft builder consider returning the prototype to its historic birthplace.

Would it not be marvellous, I submitted, to return W 4050 to Salisbury Hall? Spontaneously and with characteristic enthusiasm Sir Geoffrey agreed. In 1938, as he told me, he had rebuffed the Air Ministry's caustic rejection of his concept of a 'wooden speed bomber' with a brisk, 'we'll do it anyway'. Still decisive and adventurous, he authorised the restoration of W 4050 from a dismantled airframe at the back of a hangar and the return of the aircraft to Salisbury Hall.

Forty-two years on Philip J. Birtles, chairman of the de Havilland Museum Trust, drew back the doors of the surplus Robin hangar we had bought in 1959 with money donated by a multitude of Mosquito aircrew, industry and friends among the public. And there she was – W 4050 being readied for a celebration at the end of August, 2000, of the 60th anniversary of the Wooden Wonder's maiden flight.

Inevitably, she is showing her age and while a makeover would see her presentable for the anniversary party, plans are advanced for an army of volunteers assembled from a mix of industry and service organisations to dismantle, rebuild and re-paint her under a programme which may take several years. Work will be led by members of the DH Technical School Old Boys and Hatfield Aviation Associates (retired Hatfield managers).

W 4050 will remain at Salisbury Hall where visitors can see work in progress and, far from being deprived of a complete Mosquito, view the collection's B.Mk 35, TA 634 looking as though she is ready for an operational sortie.

Following further restoration since the most recent update on preserved Mosquitos (Appendix 5) this aircraft has been finished in the markings of No 571 Squadron in the Light Night Striking Force based at Graveley near Huntingdon.

The acquisition and exhibition of Mosquitos and associated hardware, memorabilia and photographs remained central to the museum's purpose until 1974 when the de Havilland Museum Trust was formed with the object of broadening the collection, purchasing land to permit expansion and providing additional hangar space.

With the passing of the years the Trust's directors, dependent upon the dedicated and indispensable assistance and labour of some 700 supporters, have created more a de Havilland Heritage Centre than a museum. Rather than record additions to the collection since the appendices were last amended I will note them here.

Symbolising the change of title many new exhibits extend what began as a memorial to the Mosquito to a commemoration of the old de Havilland magic. Pre-war exhibits include a Hornet Moth and parts of a Dragon Rapide while a Comet 1a fuselage and Vampire partially represent jet age developments.

An area designated the Halford Collection commemorates the contribution of the incomparable de Havilland engineer Frank Halford and his engines; from the Gipsy piston engine to the Vampire goblin and Comet Ghost jets and on to de Havilland Sprite and Spectre rocket engines. It also includes a library which is available for research and is especially appreciated by students of aeronautical engineering.

In more detail Salisbury Hall additions are:

DH82a Tiger Moth G-ANRX. Representing the renowned elementary trainer on which so many 1939–45 pilots learned to fly, this aircraft served at flying schools from 1939 until 1945. In 1955 it was converted for crop dusting. It was delivered to the museum in 1976.

DH82b Queen Bee LF789. Developed before the war from the Tiger Moth for use as a pilotless radio controlled target for naval and coastal guns, this example was given to the museum in 1986 and subsequently restored as the only true Queen Bee.

DH87b Hornet Moth G-ADOT. An example of the company's first cabin tourer-trainer with unusual side-by-side seating. Flew coastal patrols in 1940 and served afterwards as a communications aircraft. Sold in 1946 as a club aircraft and retired in the 1960s to a Norfolk orchard as a present for a boy. Restored by Hatfield apprentices for the museum in the early 1970s G-ADOT was rebuilt to static condition by 1988.

DH89 Dragon Rapide G-AKDW was built by Brush at Loughborough as a military Dominie and converted before service in 1945 to a civil Dragon Rapide. It was purchased by British Overseas Airways Corporation (BOAC) and leased to Iraqi Airways. Returning home, the Rapide joined British European Airways (BEA) Highlands and Islands service on 1947.

In 1949 the aircraft moved to Short's at Rochester and in 1958 was sold on to Avionics at Croydon and exported within a month to Belgium, where it was sold to Aero-Sud in France, ending up in Amsterdam as a museum piece. Finally, the Rapide was swapped in 1993 by Salisbury Hall for a partially restored Be.2e with the aim of restoration to flying condition.

DH94 Moth Minor G-AFOJ. Completed at Hatfield in the summer of 1949, this aircraft was employed by the company on communications flying and testing variable pitch airscrews. In 1949 it transferred to the London Flying Club at Panshanger. After several moves G-AFOJ was based at an Essex farm whence it last flew in 1969. Stored in a barn, it was collected by the museum in 1991.

DH100 Vampire FB.6 J-1008. Built at Hatfield in 1949 for Switzerland, where it served with three fighter squadrons and as an advanced trainer before donation in 1974 to the museum, where it is preserved in complete condition.

DH104 Dove D-IFSB and Dove 8 G-AREA. The first of these Doves served in Germany on calibration and communications work from 1955 to 1976 and in 1978 was offered to the museum. The second Dove was also built at Chester and was employed from 1961 as a company demonstrator afterwards joining the Hawker Siddeley, later British Aerospace flight communications fleet, as a VIP six seater. Destined for the museum, it was stored in 1991 at Hatfield Aerodrome.

DH Comet 1a, 2R and Srs4. Representing the de Havilland jet airliner heritage, this collection includes an Air France Comet fuselage, the nose of a Comet 2 spy-in-the-sky jet and a former Dan-Air Comet 4 flight simulator.

DH110 Sea Vixen FAW.2 XJ565. Designed as a naval all weather fighter, this example was delivered in 1960 as a Mk.1 and converted to a Mk.2 and flew with a variety of Fleet Air Arm squadrons and was used subsequently for development. It was retired in 1976 when it was moved to the museum and exhibited with the markings of 899 Squadron with which it served in the aircraft carrier *Eagle*. It has working wing-fold hydraulics.

DH112 Venom NF.3 WX853. Issued to No 23 Squadron in 1955 and served until 1957 when it was used for ground instruction and later as gate guardian at RAF Debden. Delivered to Salisbury Hall in 1968, it bears 23 Squadron markings.

DH112 Venom FB.4 WR539. Issued in 1957 to No 60 Squadron at Tengah, Singapore, serving afterwards with No 28 Squadron in Hong Kong. In 1962 it flew the RAF's last Venom sortie. Following gate duties this aircraft was repatriated and finally arrived at the museum for major restoration.

DH112 Sea Venom FAW.22. Served initially with No 891 Squadron from 1957 and No 894 Squadron from 1960 before storage and issue in 1965 to Airwork. From 1970 FAW 22 was on static display at the School of Maritime Operations, *Dryad* whence it joined the museum in 1978 and was fully restored in the markings of 894 Squadron and with folding wings.

DH113 Vampire NF.10 WM729. Issued to No 151 Squadron at West Malling in 1953, moving in 1955 to No 2 Air Navigation School and sold as scrap in 1959 although the fuselage pod survived and was presented by Alan Allen to the museum in 1994. This exhibit completed Salisbury Hall's collection of seven de Havilland jet fighters.

DH114 Heron 2D G-AOTI. Developed as a larger Dove, this aircraft was a Highlands and Islands feeder airliner with BEA from 1956 to 1969, when it was acquired by Rolls-Royce, moving to Aces High, Fairoaks, in 1982 and Top Flight at Exeter in 1985. Stored in the open at Biggin Hill from 1988, G-AOTI was acquired by the museum in 1995 where restoration began in Rolls-Royce livery.

DH115 Vampire T.11 XJ772 was delivered in 1952 to the Royal Norwegian Air Force, which in 1955 gave it to the RAF, where it was employed as a trainer until retirement to Brooklands College in 1971. It was donated to the museum in 1994.

DH121 Trident Two and Three. Originated by de Havilland, the Trident series was inherited by Hawker Siddeley Aviation following the 1959 merger. Salisbury Hall's Trident Two flew with BEA from 1968 to 1981 and was scrapped in 1982, when the nose and front cabin were donated to the museum. The airliner's radios are in working order. The Three joined BEA in 1972 and was withdrawn in 1986 after flying the last Trident Manchester-Heathrow shuttle but made a final flight back to its birthplace at Hatfield. It was also the last Trident flight other than in China. It was presented to the museum in 1993 as an essential de Havilland heritage exhibit.

DH125 G-ARYC. Last of the illustrious line bearing DH initials and first known as the Jet Dragon, this exhibit is an example of the company's private venture project for a six seater business aircraft powered by a pair of Bristol Siddeley Viper engines. It was used from 1963 as a flying testbed for the Viper, moving on in 1966 as a communications link between Filton, Bristol, and Toulouse in support of the Concorde programme. Donated by Rolls-Royce, it was reassembled at the museum in 1979.

DHC1 Chipmunk T.10 WP790. This aircraft was the first Chester-built production example of the first aircraft to be developed solely by the de Havilland Aircraft Company of Canada to replace the Tiger Moth as a standard basic trainer. Powered by a de Havilland Gipsy Major 8 and delivered in 1952 to No 17 Reserve Flying School at Hornchurch, it served a succession of flying schools until 1973, being donated the next year to the museum. The first aircraft to be restored by Salisbury Hall supporters, WP790 carries the markings of Birmingham University Air Squadron in which it once served.

Cierva C.24 Autogiro G-ABLM. Possibly the collection's most unusual exhibit this Autogiro, while ascribed to its designer, Don Juan de la Cierva, was produced by de Havilland in 1931 with a cabin similar to that of the Puss Moth and powered by a Gipsy 111 engine. It was entered in the Brooklands to Newcastle Air Race in 1932 and flown by Reggie Brie at an average speed of 103.5 mph. Donated to the Science Museum in 1935, where it was stored unseen until 1951 when it was displayed at a Hendon fifty years of flying exhibition. Subsequently G-ABLM was restored by Hatfield apprentices and loaned permanently by the Science Museum.

Airspeed AS.58 Horsa Glider. Recalling D-Day and other Second World War airborne exploits, this welcome if unexpected exhibit owes its presence to the de Havilland takeover of Airspeed from Swan Hunter in the 1930s and the building of the first two Horsa gliders at Salisbury Hall. As with the Mosquito, the Horsa was built mainly of wood. This Horsa's fuselage and nose arrived at the museum in 1975 after garaging an MG in a Banbury field. The exhibit has been adopted by the Glider Regiment Pilot Association.

Appendix 1
The de Havilland Mosquito (DH98)

The de Havilland Mosquito was an all-wood mid-wing monoplane powered by two Rolls-Royce Merlin engines with de Havilland hydromatic three-blade airscrews. Armour plate was provided for the crew, and the canopy was a welded steel structure, entirely covered with Perspex with the exception of the bulletproof windscreen.

The fuselage was of oval, tapering cross-section and was made of balsa wood sandwiched between plywood sheeting, so forming a monocoque with occasional wood bulkheads. On the fighter versions the crew entry was through a door on the starboard side of the cockpit, and in the bomber and PRU versions through a door in the bottom of the fuselage. A hatch behind the wing, on the starboard side of the fuselage, gave access to the compartments in the rear of the fuselage, where radio, desert equipment etc. were stowed.

The DH98 Mosquito war machine, of which 7,781 were built.

The wing was a one-piece cantilever structure consisting of two wooden box spars extending over the full span, with stressed plywood skin covering, reinforced by spanwise spruce stringers. Ten bullet-proofed fuel tanks were housed within the wing, and were accessible via detachable panels in the underside which formed part of the stressed skin. Slotted, hydraulically operated, ply-covered flaps, and slotted, metal-covered ailerons were fitted. The wing was attached to the fuselage by four main bolts, and by additional bolts passing through the flanges of the inner ribs.

The tail plane and fin were cantilever, all-wood structures consisting of two box spars and stressed plywood skins. The elevator and rudder were Alclad structures, the elevator being metal-covered and the rudder fabric-covered. Combined trimming and balance tabs were fitted to all control surfaces, except starboard aileron, the tab of which acted as balance only.

The alighting gear consisted of two completely interchangeable single wheel units, one under each engine nacelle, and a retractable tail-wheel unit. The undercarriage and tail

124

wheel retracted backwards under hydraulic power. The shock absorber legs were of the compression rubber type. Dunlop pneumatic brakes were fitted to the undercarriage, two brakes to each wheel. The usual indicators, warning and emergency lowering devices were fitted.

The Merlin engines were mounted on steel tube frames attached to the front spar and undercarriage fixed structure. The oil and coolant radiators for each engine were built into the wing leading-edge between the engine nacelle and the fuselage. The coolant temperature was regulated by electro-pneumatic ram-controlled flaps in the radiator duct exits. One bullet-proofed oil tank was located in each undercarriage wheel well. A hydraulic pump was fitted to each engine for alighting gear, wing flap and bomb door operation and a vacuum pump on each engine operated the gyroscopic instruments; the exhaust from the starboard pump was utilized for pressurizing the fuel tanks. The port engine drove a Heywood compressor for operating the guns, brakes, radiator cooling flaps, two-speed supercharger gear, and air intake control (the latter when fitted). Electric starters and booster coils were fitted. Automatic Graviner fire extinguishers, which could also be operated manually from the cockpit, were fitted in each engine nacelle.

Power for the electrical services was supplied by a generator of 24 volts 1500 watts driven by the starboard engine. An alternator for operating the special radio equipment was driven by the port engine. A wireless set, remote-controlled by the pilot, was installed in the rear fuselage compartment on the left-hand side. There was an intercommunication system between the pilot and observer. ARI 5083 was mounted on the front spar behind the pilot's seat.

Additional equipment included electric windscreen wiper and de-icing spray, oxygen apparatus, inflatable dinghy and the usual pyrotechnic items. The armament and bomb-load varied with the duties the aircraft was called upon to perform and are listed under the various Mark numbers (pages 125-134).

N.B. The weights and maximum dive speed quoted below are those at which the Mosquito was limited for peacetime flying in the RAF. Under wartime conditions these aircraft flew at very much higher all-up weights and hence were able to carry a much larger quantity of fuel and greater bomb load. It is considered now, however, that these high weights were not sufficiently safe for peacetime operations.

	Bomber	Fighter Bomber	Torpedo Recce
	Mk 35	Mk 6	Mk 33
Maximum all-up weight (lb.)	22,000	21,700	21,000
Span	54 ft. 2 in.	54 ft. 2 in.	54 ft. 2 in.
Gross wing area (sq. ft.)	450	450	450
Crew	2	2	2
Fuel total (gall.)	539	453	405
Oil total (gall.)	31	31	31
Wing loading (lb./sq. ft.)	49	48	47
Still air range at recommended cruising speed (miles)	1,600	1,120	930
Maximum speed at altitude in F.S. gear (m.p.h.)	425	378	387
Maximum speed at sea level (m.p.h.)	326	336	344
Initial rate of climb at sea level at full climb power (ft./min.)	2,500	1,870	1,870
Operational ceiling (ft.)	37,000	26,000	26,000
Take-off distance to 50 ft. screen from rest in still air at maximum weight (yds.)	980	900	600

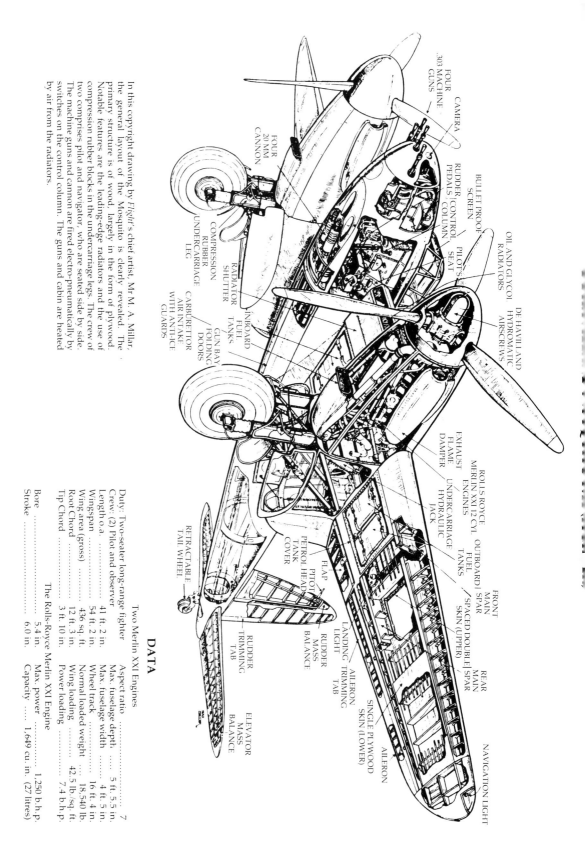

FOUR
303 MACHINE
GUNS

CAMERA

FOUR
20 MM
CANNON

RUDDER [CONTROL
PEDALS CONTROL
COLUMN]

BULLET PROOF
SCREEN

PILOT'S
SEAT

COMPRESSION
RUBBER
UNDERCARRIAGE
LEG

RADIATOR
SHUTTER

CARBURETTOR
AIR INTAKE
WITH ANTI-ICE
GUARDS

GUN BAY
FOLDING
DOORS

INBOARD
FUEL TANKS

DE HAVILLAND
HYDROMATIC
AIRSCREWS

OIL AND GLYCOL
RADIATORS

EXHAUST
FLAME
DAMPER

ROLLS ROYCE
MERLIN XXI 12 CYL.
ENGINES

UNDERCARRIAGE
HYDRAULIC
JACK

OUTBOARD
FUEL
TANKS

FRONT
MAIN
SPAR

REAR
MAIN
SPAR

SPACED DOUBLE
SKIN (UPPER)

NAVIGATION LIGHT

AILERON

SINGLE PLYWOOD
SKIN (LOWER)

AILERON
TRIMMING
TAB

LANDING
LIGHT

FLAP

PETROL HEAD
TANK
COVER

PITOT
HEAD

RUDDER
MASS
BALANCE

RUDDER
TRIMMING
TAB

ELEVATOR
MASS
BALANCE

RETRACTABLE
TAIL WHEEL

In this copyright drawing by *Flight's* chief artist, Mr M. A. Millar, the general layout of the Mosquito is clearly revealed. The primary structure is of wood, largely in the form of plywood. Notable features are the leading-edge radiators and the use of compression rubber blocks in the undercarriage legs. The crew of two comprises pilot and navigator, who are seated side by side. The machine guns and cannon are fired electro-pneumatically by switches on the control column. The guns and cabin are heated by air from the radiators.

DATA

Two Merlin XXI Engines

Duty: Two-seater long-range fighter
Crew: (2) Pilot and observer

Length o.a.	41 ft. 2 in.
Wingspan	54 ft. 2 in.
Wing area (gross)	436 sq. ft.
Root Chord	12 ft. 3 in.
Tip Chord	3 ft. 10 in.

Aspect ratio	7
Max. fuselage depth	5 ft. 5.5 in.
Max. fuselage width	4 ft. 5 in.
Wheel track	16 ft. 4 in.
Normal loaded weight	18,540 lb.
Wing loading	42.5 lb./sq. ft.
Power loading	7.4 b.h.p.

The Rolls-Royce Merlin XXI Engine

Bore	5.4 in.
Stroke	6.0 in.

Max. power	1,250 b.h.p.
Capacity	1,649 cu. in. (27 litres)

Appendix 2
The Rolls-Royce Merlin Engine

The Mosquito will always be linked with the Merlin in aeronautical history. As a fast bomber it achieved its greatest triumph when it was used to make two bombing sorties a night against Berlin, carrying 4,000 lb. of bombs on each run.

The design of the Merlin engine which made this feat possible was started late in 1932. The Rolls-Royce Company had already gained considerable knowledge of high-performance engines with the 'R' type racing engines which, powering the Supermarine S6 seaplanes in the 1929 and 1931 contests, won the Schneider Trophy outright for Great Britain and the Merlin design incorporated the lessons learnt. Initially the engine was developed as a private venture by Rolls-Royce.

The 12 cylinders were ranged in two banks of 6 cylinders cast in a single block and inclined at an angle of $60°$ to one another. Cooling also followed Rolls-Royce's practice of using liquid. The first Merlin had a single-stage supercharger and the first official 100 hours type test was completed in 1934 at a rating of 790 b.h.p. In the next year the Merlin passed a type test at 1,045 b.h.p. and this version was the first to be put into production. These early engines powered the Hurricanes and Spitfires which won the Battle of Britain.

During the late 1930s much development work was carried out to improve the altitude performance of the Merlin and a two-stage supercharger was introduced. The gain in engine power at 30,000 ft. with this supercharger was 300 b.h.p. or a gain of nearly 50% of power. The first Merlin to incorporate the two-stage supercharger was the Merlin X. The next production type engine was the Merlin XX. The two-speed supercharger of this engine was of improved design incorporating a modified form of entry which gave a freer flow of air to the supercharger, this with other detailed improvements gave the Merlin XX a rating in low gear of 1,240 b.h.p. at 2,850 r.p.m. at 10,000 ft. +9 sq. ins. boost, and the figure was 1,175 b.h.p. at 2,850 r.p.m. at 17,500 ft., again at +9 sq. ins. boost. It was these engines in the Merlin XX series that powered the Mosquito. Merlin 21's powered the Mosquitos 1, 2, 3, 4 and 6; Merlin 23's powered the Mosquitos 1, 2, 4, 6, 12 and 13; the Merlin 25 powered the Mosquitos 6 and 12.

Flight, commenting on the development of the Merlin XX series, says, 'These figures represent an increase of nearly 250 b.h.p. over the original production Merlin and illustrate in a convincing manner the technical progress achieved by years of "toil, tears and sweat". Nor is the limit of attainment yet in sight.'

Several more variants of the Merlin were used to power the Mosquito, in particular the Packard-built engine powered the Canadian-built aircraft. The last production variants of the Mosquito, the Mks. 34, 35 and 36, were fitted with the Merlin 113 and 114. These engines delivered 1,430 b.h.p. at 27,250 ft. with a boost pressure of +18 lb.

The Merlin has been described as one of the outstanding aero engines of all time: during the war more than 150,000 engines were made on both sides of the Atlantic and in addition to the Mosquito the Merlin powered the Lancaster and Mustang of later years, whilst in the early days of the war Whitleys, Beaufighters and Defiants were also Merlin-powered.

Appendix 3
The Development of the Mosquito

Type and Mark No.

P.R. Mk 1   Prototype and first few photographic-reconnaissance aircraft. Distinguishable by short engine nacelles. Two Rolls-Royce Merlin 21 engines with two-speed single-stage superchargers and de Havilland hydromatic propellers. Prototype, W.4050, was designed and built at Salisbury Hall, near St Albans, Herts, and flown from Hatfield on 25th November 1940. It was adaptable to carry four 250-lb. bombs in fuselage. First deliveries to RAF in July 1941. First operational sortie by a Mosquito was carried out in W.4055 on 18th September 1941. Tankage 690/690 gallons.[1] All-up weight, 18,050 lb.

[1] Explanation of tankage figures: the first figure is the maximum fuel load possible with all long-range tanks installed, and at the expense of useful load. The second figure is the fuel carried with maximum useful load.

N.F. Mk 2   Fighter. Four 20-mm. cannon and four ·303-in. Browning machine guns. Prototype, W.4052, first flew 15th May 1941 from meadow behind Salisbury Hall. Rolls-Royce Merlin 21 and 23 engines. First home defence night fighter squadron equipped with Mark 2 became fully operational May 1942. Two built experimentally with rotating dorsal gun turret with four ·303-in. machine guns in 1941, later converted to T. Mk 3. Fitted with A.I. Mk 4 radar, later superseded by A.I. Mk 5.

A day and night intruder adaptation (without Air Interception radar normal to the home defence fighter) was operational from July 1942. In December 1942 the first Mosquito intruder squadron went overseas — to Malta (No. 23 Squadron) — with Mk 2's and began to get F.B. Mk 6's in June 1943.

One Mk 2 was sent to Australia as a sample and was assembled and flown at the end of 1942. Its RAAF serial was A52-1001. Tankage 547/453 gallons.

T. Mk 3   Trainer. Rolls-Royce Merlin 21 and 23 engines. Like Mk 2 but with dual control and without armament. Eleven Mk 3 airframes were sent

A T.III of the Turkish Air Force. *(via Stuart Howe)*

to Australia where eight were assembled by de Havilland, Australia, and three by the RAAF. The majority were sent without engines. Packard Merlin 31 and 33 were fitted. Tankage 716/453 gallons.

T. Mk 3's supplied to the Turkish Air Force were used as bombers and carried one 500-lb. bomb under each wing.

B. Mk 4 Unarmed bomber. Like P.R. Mk 1 but with longer engine nacelles. Rolls-Royce Merlin 21 and 23 engines. Stowage for four 500-lb. bombs (with shortened vanes) in fuselage in place of four 250-lb. bombs of the original design formula. Modified later to carry 4,000-lb. bomb. First operational sorties made in daylight to Cologne. First bombing of Berlin in daylight was made by Mk 4's on 30th January 1943. 263 Mk 4's were built. Tankage 539/539 gallons.

The Pathfinder version was an RAF modification of the B. Mk 4.

All-up weight 20,900 lb.; with 4,000-lb. bomb, 22,500 lb. Tankage 497/497 gallons. Some B. Mk 4's had strengthened wing to take 50-gallon drop tanks.

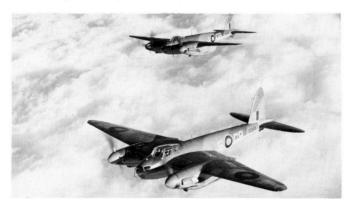

B.IV Series II Mosquitos of 105 Squadron flying out of Marham, Norfolk, in December 1942. *(Flight International)*

P.R. Mk 4 Unarmed photographic-reconnaissance aircraft. Like B. Mk 4, but with provision for cameras instead of bomb load. Tankage 690/539 gallons. All-up weight 19,050 lb.

Variant of Mk 4 was supplied to BOAC as the prototype Mosquito courier-transport. 'Accommodation' for two passengers on their backs in felt-padded bomb bay.

B. Mk 5 Prototype developed from B. Mk 4, with new 'standard wing' to take two 50-gallon jettisonable wing tanks or two 500-lb. wing bombs. Rolls-Royce Merlin 23 engines. Basis of Canadian B. Mk 7.

FB.VI NT137 of 418 (City of Edmonton) Squadron (RCAF) at Hurn, 22nd July 1944.
(Public Archives of Canada)

F.B. Mk 6   Developed from Mk 2 as B. Mk 5 was developed from B. Mk 4. Fighter bomber with Rolls-Royce Merlin 21, 23 and 25 engines. Same armament as Mk 2 fighter plus two 50-gallon jettisonable wing tanks or two 500-lb. wing bombs (or extra tankage in fuselage behind the cannon). Total bomb load 2,000 lb. Tankage 716/453 gallons. All-up weight 22,000 lb.

In action in Europe early 1943 and South-East Asia late 1943.

Provision was made in 1944 for carrying four rocket projectiles with 60-lb. heads under each wing in place of wing tanks or bombs — for attacks on submarines and shipping.

Some Mk 6's were modified for minelaying.

Two Mk 6 Mosquitos modified for deck landing and converted to Sea Mosquitos by adding an arrester hook, strengthening the fuselage and fitting four-blade propellers. They became the basis of Mk 33. The second of these aircraft had manually operated folding wings.

Eight unarmed Mk 6's supplied to BOAC.

B. Mk 7   *See Canadian Production.*

P.R. Mk 8   First high-altitude Mosquitos. Converted from B. Mk 4 by fitting special Merlin 61 intercooled engines with two-speed, two-stage superchargers and providing for two 50-gallon jettisonable wing tanks. Only five built. Tankage 860/539 gallons. All-up weight 21,400 lb.

B. Mk 9   First high-altitude unarmed bomber. Merlin 72 inter-cooled engines (12-lb. boost for take-off, maximum boost 18 lb.) with two-speed, two-stage superchargers. No pressure cabin. Four 500-lb. bombs in fuselage, two 500-lb. bombs on wings. Extra fuselage tanks and 50-gallon wing drop tanks alternative to bombs. All converted in 1944 to take one 4,000-lb. bomb in fuselage with two 50-gallon wing drop tanks. 100-gallon wing drop tanks substituted later in 1944 subject to weight limitation on 25,200 lb. Tankage 860/539 gallons.

First daylight raid on Germany with 4,000-lb. bombs — Duisburg, 29th November 1944. Tankage 697/497 gallons.

All-up weight 22,850 lb. With 4,000-lb. bomb and 50-gallon drop tanks, 24,900 lb. With 4,000-lb. bomb and 100-gallon drop tanks, 25,200 lb.

A Pathfinder version was developed by the RAF.

P.R. Mk 9   Photographic-reconnaissance version of B. Mk 9. Range over 2,000 miles. Used by RAF and U.S. 8th Air Force for meteorological reconnaissance over Europe before all major day and night bombing assaults. Tankage 860/539 gallons. All-up weight 22,000 lb.

F.B. Mk 10   Proposed fighter bomber as F.B. Mk 6 but with Merlin 67 engines. Never built.

Mk. 11   (Number never used.)

N.F. Mk 12   Four-cannon fighter developed from and similar to Mk 2 but with centimetric A.I. Mk 8 radar in a nose radome in place of A.I. Mk 5, and four machine guns. 97 Mk 2's converted to N.F. Mk 12's. The strengthened B. Mk 5 type wing was not fitted. Tankage 507/403 gallons. All-up weight, 18,720 lb. Merlin 21 and 23 engines.

Leavesden-built NF.XIII of 29 Squadron with a thimble nose housing AI Mk. VIII radar. It had a top speed of 394 m.p.h. and could carry either drop tanks or a bomb load, as well as its normal armament of four 20 mm. cannon. HK428 was scrapped in September 1946.
(via Stuart Howe)

N.F. Mk 13   Four-cannon fighter developed from F.B. Mk 6. Merlin 21 and 23 engines. Four machine guns replaced by A.I. Mk 8 radar in 'bull' nose. 270 were built. All-up weight 21,000 lb. Tankage 716/453 gallons.

N.F. Mk 14   Proposed fighter as Mk 13 but with high-altitude Merlin 67 engines. Never built.

N.F. Mk 15   Special high-altitude fighter developed urgently in seven days from pressure cabin prototype P.R. Mk 8 with extended wing tips, reduced fuel tankage, reduced armour, four ·303-in. machine guns in blister under fuselage. Only five built. Tankage 335/335 gallons. All-up weight 17,600 lb.

B. Mk 16   Pressure cabin development of B. Mk 9 with Merlin 72, 73, 76 and 77 engines, 3,000 lb. of bombs. All converted in 1944 to take 4,000-lb. bomb in fuselage and two 50-gallon wing drop tanks, or 100-gallon drop tanks with four 500-lb. bombs. Marshall cabin supercharger

B.XVI ML926/G fitted with a radar bomb-sight and Oboe repeater at H2S trials at Defford.
(via Stuart Howe)

maintained 2¾ lb./sq. ft. above outside atmosphere, equivalent to about 10,000 feet less altitude. Maximum take-off weight, 20,200 lb.; maximum landing weight, 20,500 lb. Tankage 860/539 gallons with 500-lb. bombs, 597/497 gallons with 4,000-lb. bomb.

A Pathfinder version was developed by the RAF.

Some B. Mk 16's were fitted with H2S radomes. Several in service with BAFO after the war were fitted with cameras. One B. Mk 16 was fitted with four-blade Rotol airscrews and used for testing by Rotal Ltd. In 1947 the B. Mk 16 was used as a launching platform for Vickers-Armstrong pilotless remote-controlled, rocket-propelled, supersonic models. 459 B. Mk 16's were produced by de Havilland and 250 by Percival Aircraft.

Tankage 860/539 gallons with four 500-lb. bombs, 596/497 gallons with one 4,000-lb. All-up weight 25,200 lb.

Nearest the camera is PR.XVI RF973 of the French Air Force flying over the Algerian coast. *(via Francis Bergesé and Stuart Howe)*

P.R. Mk 16   Photographic-reconnaissance version of B. Mk 16. Three extra fuel tanks carried in bomb bay. In addition to the cameras carried in the fuselage, one F.52 camera could be carried in each drop tank. 432 were built. Tankage 860/539 gallons. All-up weight 22,350 lb.

About 19 of these aircraft were bought complete by the RAAF.

N.F. Mk 17   Fighter developed from, and similar to, Mk 12 with American A.I. Mk 10 radar. One hundred conversions from Mk 12. Tankage 547/403 gallons. All-up weight 20,400 lb.

F.B. Mk 18   The Tsetse. Development from F.B. Mk 6 with nose modified to take an adaptation of the six-pounder (57 mm.) anti-tank gun instead of four 20-mm. cannon. Four ·303-in. machine guns retained. The six-pounder could fire 25 shells in 20 seconds. Merlin 25 engines. 27 were converted from F.B. Mk 6. Crew and engines heavily armour-plated. 50-gallon or 100-gallon drop tanks or 500-lb. wing bombs or eight 60-lb. rocket projectiles. Used mainly by Coastal Command against submarines and shipping. First action, 4th November 1943.

Tankage 668/403 gallons.

N.F. Mk 19   Fighter developed from, and similar to, Mk 13 but with Merlin 25 engines and able to take either American or British radar equipment (American A.I. Mk 10 or British A.I. Mk 8). 220 were built. In 1948-49 forty-five were overhauled by Fairey Aviation and supplied to the Royal Swedish Air Force, who designated the aircraft the J.30. Four-blade airscrews were fitted to the Swedish aircraft.

Tankage 716/453 gallons. All-up weight 21,750 lb.

An NF.XIX of the Swedish Air Force. *(via Stuart Howe)*

Mks 20 to 29	*See Canadian Production.*
N.F. Mk 30	Fighter developed from Mk 19 with high-altitude Merlin 72 (first 70 aircraft) 76 and 113 engines. No pressure cabin: Tankage 716/453 gallons. All-up weight 22,700 lb.

An NF.30 of the Belgian Air Force. *(via Stuart Howe)*

Mk 31	This Mark number was reserved for a Packard Merlin-engined night-fighter version which was never built.
P.R. Mk. 32	Specially lightened variant of P.R. Mk 16 with Merlin 113 and 114 two-stage supercharged engines, with extended wing tips for high-altitude operation. Crew armour plate deleted. No self-sealing tanks and reduced photographic equipment.
T.R. Mk 33	Fleet Air Arm version developed from F.B. Mk 6 for fighting, bombing, torpedo-carrying and photographic reconnaissance. Merlin 25 engines. Manually operated folding wings. Pneumatic landing gear with smaller wheels. American radar in 'thimble' radome replaced the four machine guns. Four 20-mm. cannon. Two 500-lb. bombs or 50- or

Ratings of 811 Squadron FAA pushing out a TR.33 at HMS Peregrine, Ford, in Sussex in November 1945.
(David Hughes, via Stuart Howe)

A close-up of the 18-inch torpedo under TR.33 LR387, the second prototype, converted from an FB.VI with folding wings, ASH radar and four-blade propellers.
(British Aerospace)

30-gallon drop tanks or four rockets under wings; two 500-lb. bombs stowed internally or one 18-in. torpedo, mine or 2,000-lb. bomb carried under the fuselage. The first 13 production aircraft had fixed wings and rubber-in-compression shock absorbers. Span folded, 27 ft. 3 ins. Height folded, 13 ft. 6 ins. The wing folding mechanism entailed weight penalty of 300 lb.

One of the two BEA Mosquitos used for guest research at Cranfield.
(British Airways, via Stuart Howe)

P.R. Mk 34   Very long-range development of P.R. Mk 16 with Merlin 113 and 114 two-stage supercharged engines. Tankage 1,267 gallons (including two 200-gallon wing drop tanks). Still air range at 30,000 feet with no allowance for climb etc., 3,500 miles at 315 m.p.h. Pressurized cabin. Two Mk 34's were used by the BEA Gust Research Unit. This was the fastest version of the Mosquito and was capable of 422 m.p.h. in level flight.

P.R. Mk 34a   Modernized by Marshalls of Cambridge. Revised cockpit layout. One fitted with speeded undercarriage. Merlin 114A engines.
                  High-altitude development of B. Mk 16 with Merlin 113 and 114 two-stage supercharged engines. 4,000-lb. bomb with 50-gallon wing drop tanks (or 100-gallon wing tanks with four 500-lb. bombs).

T.T. Mk 35   Target towers modified from B. Bk 35's.

TT.35 of 3 CAACU, Exeter, in the early 1960s. *(via Stuart Howe)*

N.F. Mk 36   Higher-powered development of N.F. Mk 30 with Merlin 113 engines. American A.I. Mk 10 fitted. Armed with four 20-mm. cannon. The prototype flew in May 1945.

T.R. Mk 37   Replacement of Mk 33 fitted with British ASV. Mk 13B radar in 'bull' nose similar to that of N.F. Mk 36. Four 20-mm. cannon, two 500-lb. wing bombs or 50- or 30-gallon drop tanks or up to eight rockets.

N.F. Mk 38   Similar to N.F. Mk 36. Fitted with British A.I. Mk 9 radar. In consequence the cockpit enclosure was lengthened by five inches. The last Mosquito built was an N.F. Mk 38 and was completed in November 1950. Merlin 113 and 114, or 113A and 114A engines.

As a B.XVI PF489 saw service with 105 and 608 Squadrons until passing to the Royal Navy. It was converted to a TT.39 and was used for handling trials at the A&AEE at Boscombe Down. A number of TT.39s served in other countries, including Malta.
(RAF Museum)

T.T. Mk 39   Target tower converted from B. Mk 16 by General Aircraft. The naval specification Q 19/45 called for a land-based high-speed target tower capable of towing a 32-ft. winged target at 200 knots; a 16-ft. winged target at 260 knots; a 4-ft. drag sleeve at 180 knots; or a 2-ft. drag sleeve at 260 knots. Slightly cropped 4-bladed airscrews were fitted. All-up weight 21,500 lb.

CANADIAN PRODUCTION

B. Mk 7   First 25 Canadian-built Mosquitos, based on B. Mk 5 but with Packard Merlin 31 engines (similar to V-1650-1 in American aircraft) driving Hamilton standard propellers. Considerable British equipment. First aircraft flew at Toronto on 24th September 1942. Four 500-lb. bombs stowed internally plus one 250-lb. bomb or 500-lb. bomb or 50-gallon drop tank under each wing.

B. Mk 20   Second batch of Canadian production. Similar to B. Mk 7 but with Canadian-American equipment. Packard Merlin 31 or 33 engines. First two Canadian-built Mosquitos delivered to Britain (KB162, KB328) flew via Greenland in August 1943. They were operational on 29th November 1943, in a raid on Berlin.

     Four 500-lb. bombs plus one 250-lb. or 500-lb. bomb or 50-gallon

Canadian-built B.20s after conversion for the USAAF at Niagara, N.Y. State. *(Bell Aerospace)*

drop tank. 245 were built. Forty fitted with cameras were supplied for the USAAF, who knew them as the F.8 and used them for meteorological and operational reconnaissance. All-up weight 21,980 lb. Tankage 860/539 gallons.

F.B. Mk 21	Fighter bomber corresponding to F.B. Mk 6, otherwise as B. Mk 20. Replaced by F.B. Mk 26. Only three built. Two fitted with Packard Merlin 31, one with Packard Merlin 33 engines.
T. Mk 22	Dual-control unarmed trainer developed from F.B. Mk 21. Packard Merlin 33 engines. Similar to T. Mk 3. Only four built.
B.Mk 23	High-altitude bomber, a development of the B. Mk 20 projected to make use of supplies of Packard Merlin 69 engines but not proceeded with because Packard Merlin 225 (single-stage, supercharged) engines became available in sufficient quantities.
F.B. Mk 24	High-altitude fighter bomber developed from F.B. Mk 21 with Packard Merlin 301 two-stage supercharged engines. Only one built.
B. Mk 25	Identical to B. Mk 20 but with Packard Merlin 225 (18-lb. boost) engines. All-up weight 21,980-lb. 400 built. Tankage 860/539 gallons.
F.B. Mk 26	Fighter bomber developed from F.B. Mk. 6 but with Packard Merlin 225 (18-lb. boost) engines and Canadian-American equipment. To replace F.B. Mk 21. 338 built. All-up weight 21,470 lb.
T. Mk 27	Trainer development from T. Mk 22 with Packard Merlin 225 engines (18-lb. boost).
F.B. Mk 28	Fighter bomber to succeed F.B. Mk 26. Rolls-Royce Merlin 25 engines.

A Nationalist Chinese Air Force FB.26 at Hankow in 1948. *(George Stewart, via Stuart Howe)*

B. or F.B. Mk 29   Development of B. Mk.20. Packard Merlin 33 engines. 50 built.

AUSTRALIAN PRODUCTION

F.B. Mk 40   First Australian-built batch. Fighter bomber based on F.B. Mk 6 with Hamilton Standard or Australian-built de Havilland Hydromatic propellers. First aircraft flown at Sydney, 23rd July 1943. First 100 aircraft Packard Merlin 31 engines. Subsequent aircraft, Packard Merlin 33 engines.
A total of 178 F.B. Mk 40's were built but a number of these were converted to other types. All were subsequently modified to carry 100-gallon drop tanks. Tankage 713/453 gallons.

P.R. Mk 40   Unarmed photographic conversion of the F.B. Mk 40. First to be converted was delivered on 26th May 1944. Two 100-gallon drop tanks were fitted and extra oil and oxygen carried. The camera installation consisted of one adjustable vertical camera in the nose, two fixed vertical cameras and two fixed oblique cameras in the rear fuselage. These aircraft gave notable service, carrying out mapping and reconnaissance work during the drive north from Australia in 1944. Tankage 856/539 gallons. Packard Merlin 31 engines.

P.R. Mk 41   Similar to F.B. Mk 40 with two-stage supercharged Packard 69 engines. This was a conversion from the last batch of undelivered F.B. Mk 40's and was practically identical to the Mk 40, but for extra radio equipment and the engines. Twenty-eight were built. They were used extensively until 1953 in the aerial survey of Australia. The first was delivered on 29th May 1947. A P.R. Mk 41 Mosquito was entered in the New Zealand Air Race in 1953, fitted with Merlin 77 engines to enable flight at higher altitudes. This aircraft crashed in the Indian Ocean near Burma before the race began. Tankage 856/539 gallons.

F.B. Mk 42   An F.B. Mk 40 was adapted to take the Packard Merlin 69 engine. After testing, the project was dropped and the aircraft was used as the prototype P.R. Mk 41. Apart from the engines it was very similar to the F.B. Mk 40.

T.Mk 43   A conversion of the F.B. Mk 40 and almost identical except for addition of dual control, as in the T.Mk 3, and dual elevator trim tabs. 22 were built.

Appendix 4
List of Suppliers and Contractors of the Mosquito Project

Since the Mosquito Museum was founded at Salisbury Hall additions to the collection include the following aircraft, engines and other items:

TYPE	SERIAL No.	COMMENTS
Airspeed AS.58 Horsa II	TL615	Forward fuselage only.
Bleriot XI	BAPC.105	On loan to the Aviodome.
Cierva C.24	G-ABLM	On loan from Science Museum.
DH 82A Tiger Moth	G-ANRX	N6550. On loan from Stuart Howe.
DH 82A Tiger Moth	G-ANFP	N9503. On loan from Stuart Howe.
DH 82B Queen Bee	BAPC 186	
DH 87B Hornet Moth	G-ADOT	X9326. On loan.
DH 98 Mosquito	W4050	E0234. Prototype.
DH 98 Mosquito FB.VI	TA122	Fuselage with wings of TR.33, TW233.
DH 98 Mosquito B.35	TA634	G-AWJV.
DH 98 Mosquito B.35	TJ118	Cockpit section.
DH 100 Vampire FB.6	J-1008	Ex-Swiss Air Force.
DH 103 Sea Hornet NF.21	VX250	Rear fuselage and other components.
DH 104 Dove 6	D-IFSB	N4280V, G-AMXR. On loan, Deutsches Museum.
DH 106 Comet IA	G-AOJT	F-BGNX of Air France. Fuselage only.
DH 110 Sea Vixen FAW.2	XJ565	
DH 112 Sea Venom FAW.22	XG730	
DH 112 Venom NF.3	WX853	7443M.
DH 115 Vampire T.II	XE985	With wings of WZ476.
DH 121 Trident 2E	G-AVFH	Front fuselage only.
DH 125	G-ARYC	Third prototype.
DHC.I Chipmunk T.10	WP790	Incorporates parts of G-BBNC.
Royal Aircraft Factory BE.2e	A1325	Ex-Norwegian 37, 133.
Toucan MPA	BAPC 146	Man-powered aircraft.

The engine collection includes the complete de Havilland jet range of the Gyron, Gyron Junior, Ghost and Goblin, together with a Spectre Rocket and Super Sprite, and a number of other engines and missiles. The piston range, donated by Rolls-Royce, and including examples of the sectioned showroom type, include the Gipsy I, Gipsy III, Gipsy Major, Gipsy Queen, and a working replica of Sir Geoffrey de Havilland's Iris engine. Two Gipsy Majors on stands.

The museum's full postal address is: Mosquito Aircraft Museum, Box 107, St. Albans, Herts AL2 1BU. Tel. 0727 22051. Located off Junction 22 on the M25, between South Mymms and London Colney. Open 10.30-17.30 Sundays and Bank Holiday Mondays from Easter to the end of September. Thursdays, July-September 14.00-17.30. Other times by prior arrangement. Annual air show. The museum also has a Supporters' Club which all are welcome to join. Details from the above address. The museum is now in its thirty-first year of operation and is registered as a charity.

Appendix 5
Preserved Mosquitos

by Stuart Howe

When the reader has finished this fascinating book on the history of the Mosquito, he or she would surely be left in no doubt that this was a truly remarkable aeroplane, one of the great classics of the aviation world.

Some 45 years have now passed since the war's end, so perhaps it may be wondered just how many have survived. As can be seen from this appendix a surprising number still do exist, spread over seven different countries. This is partly due to the fact that a few were still in service, carrying out second line duties such as target towing or aerial survey, up until 1963, by which time their value, at least historically, was beginning to be realized and a handful were purchased or donated to Museums. The biggest enemy to a redundant aeroplane is the scrap metal merchant, but the Mosquito being mainly constructed of wood was of no great use to them and so after taking their small metal content they were left derelict. The remains were often burnt, but a number were rescued by enthusiasts after many years in the open, and in some cases they were only just in time.

AUSTRALIA

Narellan, NSW

At the Camden Museum of Aviation in Narellan Harold Thomas is slowly rebuilding the remains of FB.VI, HR621, but he lacks most parts of the fuselage and therefore the rebuild comes low on his list of priorities, with the other aircraft in his museum requiring more urgent attention.

HR621 saw no RAF service, and was shipped with twenty-four other Mosquitos to Melbourne, on the aircraft carriers *Fencer* and *Striker*, and then flown to the RAAF base at Narromine, NSW, to join 618 Squadron. The aircraft were not operated for very long before being sold off at prices as low as A$25. After purchase, HR621 was stored in the open on a farm in Tomingley for twenty-five years, before Harold acquired the remains for his museum in 1968. Altogether he found the remains of nine Mosquitos, recovering the few useful parts from each. Although Harold has a long way to go with his Mosquito, he is determined to rebuild a complete aircraft again.

Point Cook, Victoria

Early in 1987 the Royal Australian Air Force Museum acquired PR.XVI, NS631, from the previous owners whose original idea had been to make it airworthy. However, because of the aircraft's condition, this proved to be beyond their capabilities.

NS631 was constructed at Hatfield in the summer of 1944 and was allocated for use by the RAAF in the north-west area of the Pacific to photograph Japanese-held territories. It arrived in Australia on 13th December 1944.

PR.XVI N5631/A52-600 being recovered by Pearce Dunn in 1966 after 12 years in the open. The wings and tail had been sawn off, but Pearce has all the parts in his museum at Mildura, and he is shortly rebuilding her. *(L. Butler, via Stuart Howe)*

NS631 was then allocated its RAAF serial number of A52-600, and on 1st March 1945 it was issued to No. 87 (PR) Squadron at Coomalie Creek. The Mosquito then went on to complete some twenty operational missions over Japanese territory, including Borneo, and on one mission it was used to photograph the airstrip on Lesser Natoena Island, some 150 miles from Singapore. F/O Davies flew A52-600 on five of its missions, including its last operational sortie to Sibu and back on 10th August. Its longest flight was seven hours and fifteen minutes on a sortie to Soemba piloted by F/O Henry.

The squadron moved to Parkes in NSW but when the squadron was disbanded the aircraft was flown to RAAF Station Canberra on 3rd July 1946 to help equip the Survey Flight based there. After nineteen flights in its new role in the aerial mapping of Australia, it was declared unserviceable and was allocated to the Air and Ground Radio School at Ballarat as an instructional airframe, by which time its total flying hours were 321 hours and fifty minutes.

In 1954 it was bought by Mr E. Vollaire and ended up as a plaything for his children, and some twelve years later it was acquired by Pearce Dunn of the Warbirds Aviation Museum at Mildura, where it was stored until September 1983. It was then purchased by a syndicate formed by Allen Lane, Geoff Milne and Vin Thomas and was moved to Wodonga in NSW. It is now with the RAAF Museum at Point Cook where hopefully it will be restored in the not too distant future.

Sydney, NSW

Here, the first-year apprentices of Hawker de Havilland Australia Pty Limited are carrying out an extensive restoration of PR41, A52-319, as part of their training.

This Mosquito was the third last Australian-built FB.40. Construction commenced on 27th May 1946 and it was allocated serial number A52-210. However, during construction the fuselage was modified to become a PR41 and was re-numbered A52-319.

Accepted by the RAAF on 12th February 1968, the aircraft was delivered into the charge of 2 Aircraft Depot RAAF Richmond. On 12th March the aircraft was ferried from Richmond to 3 Aircraft Depot at Archerfield, Queensland, during which flight an electrical fire occurred, and was extinguished by the pilot. From then on, only occasional flights were made, and after the last flight as an RAAF aircraft on 21st November 1949 the aircraft was placed in long term storage at Archerfield.

VH-WAD in a very sad-looking state after her sale to America fell through, and after vandals had got to her, behind the warehouse at Melbourne, circa 1974. She is now being restored by Hawker de Havilland at Sydney. *(David Kubista, via Stuart Howe)*

One of the apprentices working on the fuselage of PR.41, A52-IO53, at the Hawker de Havilland factory in Sydney. *(via Stuart Howe)*

On 3rd March 1953 the aircraft was offered for disposal and was purchased for £100 by Captain James 'Jimmy' Woods, whose intention was to enter the Mosquito in the 1953 London to Christchurch Air Race. Woods then made several flights in his Mosquito to obtain his type endorsement.

With the start of the race on 8th October, Woods was unable to find a sponsor and his entry was withdrawn. Due to its non-participation in the race the aircraft's temporary C of A was withdrawn. The aircraft never flew again, and was stored in the Department

PR.41 A52-210/VH-WAD on display with Lancaster at Perth Airport, Australia, in July 1966. *(via Leslie Hunt)*

of Civil Aviation's hangar at Perth Airport until 1961, when it was pushed outside due to outstanding hangarage fees.

After years in the open where it was subjected to vandalism, the aircraft was sold to James A. Harwood for A$6,000 in January 1969, and was dismantled for shipment to the USA. For some years there was a history of re-sales and legal wrangles, during which time the Mosquito was badly damaged, and at one point it was discovered that 234 items had been stolen from it. In an effort to save it from further damage it was encased in six tons of steel frame, and eventually reached Melbourne, where after seven years in the open it was purchased for A$21,000 by the Australian War Memorial Museum in Canberra. Hawker de Havilland offered to take on the task of rebuilding the Mosquito, but due to the lack of skilled wood-workers available today, the task of rebuilding the aircraft has taken some seven years already, but progress is steady, and we should see a complete A52-319 before long.

BELGIUM

Brussels

Located near the centre of Brussels is the Musée De L'Armée, and amongst their fascinating collection of aircraft is a unique No.30, RK952. Built at Leavesden early in 1945, it was taken on strength by the RAF on 25th May, although it did not see any squadron service and instead ended up in long term storage.

On 31st October 1951, RK952 became one of a batch of twenty-four NF 30's that were sold to the Belgian Air Force. It was delivered in the summer of 1953 after overhaul by Fairey Aviation at Ringway and was given the BAF serial of MB-24. As soon as MB-24 arrived in Belgium all of the other NF30's were grounded due to excessive wear on their engine bearers and undercarriages. However, MB-24 had already been modified and while the others were stored, it was flying with No. 10 Squadron, No. 1 Wing, at Beauvechain. It was coded 'ND-N' and was used for radar and calibration flights and as a target aircraft for the Squadron's Meteors.

The Musée de L'Armées unique NF.30 RK952/MB24 in Brussels, July 1970. *(Stuart Howe)*

MB-24 was retired from active service on 17th October 1956, and apart from an outing to Koksijde for repainting, it has been in Brussels ever since. In recent years, members of the museum have refurbished MB-24 to superb condition, with some of the missing items found and fitted to the aircraft. The writer supplied the museum with a set of exhaust pipes that were peculiar to the NF30 in exchange for a pair of Mosquito drop-tanks for the Mosquito Aircraft Museum.

CANADA

Calgary, Alberta

At the Aero Space Museum at Calgary airport B.35, RS700/CF-HMS, is stored pending a full restoration. Built by Airspeed at Christchurch early in 1946, RS700 was flown into storage until it was sent to Leavesden on 7th February 1951 for conversion to PR.35 standards. After this work was completed, it was delivered to No. 58 Squadron at Benson on 31st March 1952, with whom it served for two years.

In 1954 RS700 was put up for disposal and was one of ten Mosquitos bought by the Canadian survey company, Spartan Air Services Ltd. Each of these Mosquitos was

B.35 RS700 in store at Calgary, Alberta, in Canada. Note the tail surfaces on the right
hand wall with the wing below. She is scheduled for eventual rebuild to flying condition.
(via Stuart Howe)

prepared for its new owners by Derby Aviation Ltd at Burnaston, and RS700 was
allocated the Canadian civil registration of CF-HMS. Delivery pilot Peter Nock flew
CF-HMS from Prestwick, via Keflavik, Narssarssuag, Goose Bay and on to Spartan's base
at Uplands Airport, Ottawa, on 17th July in a total flight time of thirteen hours and forty-
five minutes. CF-HMS was in fact the last of Spartan's ten Mosquitos to be delivered.

Spartan modified the Mosquito to carry three crew, the pilot, navigator and camera
operator, and further mods included fitting a new perspex nose cone, a redesigned
cockpit canopy and the fitting of an additional tank in the bomb bay. A Swiss-built Wild
RC-8 camera was mounted on the floor in the fuselage which shoots through a perspex
panel. A new oxygen system was installed as well as additional radio and navigational
aids.

CF-HMS was bought by private interests in 1964, and in 1972 it was donated to the
Centennial Planetarium Museum (now Aero Space Museum) and has remained in store
ever since, dismantled but in very good condition. At the time of writing it was due to
move away for restoration to start.

Edmonton, Alberta

At the City of Edmonton Artefacts Centre, another ex-Spartan Mosquito B.35, VP189/
CF-HMQ, is stored. Constructed by Airspeed at Christchurch in 1947, VP189 ended up
in long term storage at No. 22 MU, Silloth, until purchased by Spartan in December 1954.

Like all the other Spartan Mosquitos, VP189 was refurbished by Derby Aviation at
Burnaston, with David Ogilvy doing most of the test flying. Peter Nock delivered the
Mosquito to Uplands Airport on 10th June 1955, by which time it had been put on the
Canadian civil register as CF-HMQ.

Spartan also carried out survey contracts outside Canada. CF-HMQ was ferried out to
Kenya in October 1957 by Peter Nock.

CF-HMQ's last flight was on 7th October 1963 to Spartan's base at Ottawa, where it

B.35 VP189/CF-HMQ is seen here in the workshop of Bill Harvey at Chipman, near
Edmonton. She bears the legend 'Pappy Yokum' on her nose. *(via Stuart Howe)*

joined CF-HML outside the hangar until September 1967, when it was bought by Colonel J. K. Campbell and presented to No. 418 (City of Edmonton) Squadron RCAF Reserve. After restoration, CF-HMQ was placed on the gate of CFB Edmonton, but after eighteen months the weather and vandals had caused so much damage to the Mosquito that it was removed to a warehouse in Edmonton, where some restoration work was carried out. The warehouse was soon required for other purposes and the Mosquito was moved to an old barn at Chipman, Alberta.

During the winter of 1975, CF-HMQ was donated to the City of Edmonton and is now in store in the Artefacts Centre, awaiting much needed attention, which we can only hope it will get in the not too distant future.

Mission, British Columbia

The remains of B.35, TA717 are currently with Mike Meeker. Built at Hatfield in 1945, the aircraft was delivered to No. 44 MU at Edzell on 7th July. After being damaged it was repaired by Martin Hearn at Hooton Park in 1948, and was delivered to No. 15 MU at Wroughton. It was sold in May 1956 to Cloux Clan Imports in the USA and was flown to Mexico as HB-TOX for the first aerial reconnaissance work to be undertaken in Mexico. It also carried previously the American civil registration N6867C.

Mike Meeker transported B.35 TA717/XB-TOX from Mexico City to Canada in August 1979. After many years of neglect, this is the sad-looking condition he found her in.
(via Stuart Howe)

Due to an ownership dispute the Mosquito ended up behind the Holiday Inn in Mexico City, where it was allowed to rot, and in 1979 it was purchased by Mike Meeker. However, by this time the aircraft was in very poor condition, and literally fell apart when Mike started to dismantle the aircraft. The remains are now stored at his workshop in Mission, British Columbia, and it is unlikely that the aircraft will be rebuilt, but until the author obtains confirmation of this, it is still listed as a survivor.

VR796/CF-HML

Also in Mike Meeker's workshop is Mosquito B.35, VR796/CF-HML, which is being worked on so it may fly again.

Built by Airspeed at Christchurch in late 1947, this aircraft saw no operational service and was sold to Spartan Air Services in 1954 for the sum of Canadian $1,500, and after overhaul by Derby Aviation Ltd it was delivered to Uplands Airport on 3rd May 1955, the first of Spartan's ten Mosquitos (others were also bought by Spartan, but remained in Britain as sources of spares). Besides the usual survey mods, Spartan also equipped CF-HML with dual controls for pilot training. After much use, CF-HML was retired to

Here, in Don Campbell's workshop in Kapuskasing, Ontario, Canada, is B.35 VR796/CF-HML. At this stage the fuselage was on cradles between a gantry while clear dope was applied to the new fabric. Note the tailplane on the left of picture, and the wing in a bay on the right. *(via Stuart Howe)*

Ottawa in June 1963, although it was not withdrawn from the civil register until 1967.

In 1966, CF-HML was purchased by F/O Don Campbell of Kapuskasing, Ontario, for rebuilding to flying condition by his Air Cadets of No. 647 Squadron, RCAC Kapuskasing. With the Mosquito protected by thick plastic sheeting, the Cadets set about constructing a building in which to house it, and by the end of 1967 the Mosquito was safely under cover.

In September, 1968, the Canadian DoT re-allocated the Mosquito's original civil markings of CF-HML, and upon inspecting the wing structure found that the primary structure was good, with no indication of glue separation. The interior of the fuselage was completely stripped of all fittings and equipment, whereupon the interior plywood skin was inspected and re-protected. Externally, the skin was good but some of it had to be replaced, especially around the dinghy hatch. The top surface of the wing had suffered the most and had to be replaced, not a very easy task as the glue had not separated. The Cadets therefore had to pick off the upper skin inch by inch.

Due to the climatic problems at Kapuskasing, when weather conditions limited work to just a few months each year, the project was still some way from completion, so in 1979 an arrangement was made between Don Campbell and Mike Meeker of Mission, B.C., for the Mosquito to be transported to Mission for completion.

By 1984 the Mosquito was structurally complete, and the remaining tasks centred around the refitting of the electrics, hydraulics and mechanical components, as well as the overhaul of the two Merlin engines. At the moment, the project is weathering a period when funds are in short supply, but hopefully it will not be too long before we will see this Mosquito in the air once again. Many people have helped make this project possible, but were it not for the determined efforts of Don Campbell, this Mosquito may well not have existed today.

Rockliffe, Ontario

Here in the National Aeronautical Collection is the much admired Canadian-built B.XX, KB336. This Mosquito was destined not to join its counterparts in Britain and when it left the Downsview production line in June 1944 it was flown straight into storage with Eastern Air Command at Halifax. The records state that KB336 was transferred to No. 3 Repair Depot at Moncton N.B. on 22 June 1945. However, it was clearly at Moncton well before this date, for George Stewart was instructing on Mosquitos at No. 8 OTU at RCAF Greenwood, Nova Scotia, when he was asked to fly over to Moncton to pick up KB336 on

B.XX KB336 at the National Aeronautical Collection, Rockliffe, in June 1982. *(Stuart Howe)*

the 16th April, and to fly it back to Greenwood. KB336's training role didn't last very long, as it was delivered back to Moncton on 30th June, again by George Stewart.

In 1946, KB336 was allocated to No. 402 Squadron based at Winnipeg, but after delivery, the squadron was first issued with Harvards and then with Vampires. The Mosquito remained at Winnipeg for several years in the back of one of the hangars and in 1951 it was dismantled and taken into storage at Chater, Manitoba. By now, KB336 had been earmarked for preservation and on 6th February 1964 it was transferred to Rockcliffe to join the National Aeronautical Collection being set up there. At the time of writing, the NAC was being moved into new premises at Rockliffe, and no doubt KB336 will once again become one of the star attractions.

Surrey, British Columbia

Canadian-built FB.26, KA114, is in store here with the Canadian Museum of Flight and Transportation, under the watchful eye of the museum's founder, Ed Zalesky. KA114 was built early in 1945 and, apart from a brief stay with No. 7 OTU at Debart, Nova Scotia, it remained in store throughout its service life. In April 1948 it was put up for disposal and was bought by a farmer. The airframe was transported to his farm near Milo, Alberta, where it remained for the next thirty years until Ed Zalesky heard about its existence and negotiated its release to the CMFT. The aircraft was minus its engines and undercarriages, but was otherwise fairly complete. However, the fuselage was in poor condition and broke in two when being lifted onto Ed's trailer. The wing is in a much better condition, but because of CMFT's many other commitments, work has still to commence on the reconstruction of KA114.

FB.26 KA114 as found by Ed Zalesky on a farm in Alberta, Canada, before recovery to his museum in Surrey, British Columbia. Note the large hole in the fuselage. *(via Stuart Howe)*

FB.VI NZ2328 of 75 Squadron at Ohakea, New Zealand, in 1948, the fuselage of which
still survives with the Ferrymead Aeronautical Society in Christchurch.
(RNZAF, via Stuart Howe)

NEW ZEALAND

Christchurch

In 1952 Bruce Goodwin, who lived at Pigeon Bay near Christchurch, bought Mosquito
FB.VI, NZ2382/HR339, as surplus from RNZAF Wigram and, after dismantling the
aircraft, he moved it to his home. Bruce carefully stored all of the small items in his shed
with the exception of the wings, which remained outside under trees. The forward
fuselage he gave away to his neighbours for the children to play in. Here the remains
stayed until 1970 when they were re-discovered by Philip and David Ferguson, both
members of the local aviation historical society. Bruce said that they could have the
remains, providing they went to a good home. The aviation society didn't want anything
to do with the physical side of preservation, so some of the members got together and
formed the Ferrymead Aeronautical Society.

HR339 served with No. 487 (RNZAF) Squadron at Thorney Island, joining them on 23
November 1944 and no doubt it took part in many of their intruder sorties over Europe.
Eventually, HR339 was put into store and was allocated to New Zealand, leaving
Pershore for the long ferry flight on 16th October 1947. After arrival, HR339 was allotted
its new serial of NZ2382 and was delivered to Wigram. Possibly it was damaged here, for
it became an instructional airframe.

The FAS now had to find a fuselage. In the 1950s many of the Mosquitos supplied to
New Zealand were stored at Woodbourne and were eventually sold as scrap to whoever
wanted them. In late 1955 Jas W. Clarke was leader of a syndicate which bought Mosquito
NZ2328/TE758, and after being dismantled the Mosquito was transported to his farm at
Totar, near Oamaru. Here the Mosquito stayed until its remains, which included the
fuselage, were acquired by the FAS in 1972. TE758 did not see any operational service and
was sold to New Zealand, arriving on 3rd April 1947. It joined No. 75 Squadron at
Ohakea where it became the C.O.'s aircraft.

The fuselage of FB.VI TE758/NZ2328 as found by the Ferrymead Aviation Society on
J. Clarke's farm at Oamaru, which they subsequently rescued. It is now stored in
Christchurch. *(Dave Ferguson)*

Although some work has been carried out by the FAS on their Mosquito, major restoration is awaiting larger premises, but the aircraft is safe, and the FAS is to be congratulated on its fine efforts in ensuring that this Mosquito was saved.

Mapua

Here, in good condition, is FB.VI, TE910/NZ2336. Built by Standard Motors at Coventry in October 1945, it was flown straight into store with No. 27 MU at Shawbury until it was bought by the New Zealand Government in November 1946. TE910 left for New Zealand from Pershore on 6th December, arriving on 24th April. It was then allocated its new serial number NZ2336 and was put into long term storage, emerging in November 1951 to join No. 75 Squadron at Ohakea. In April 1952 it was again put into storage at Woodbourne, by which time it had flown only eighty hours and thirty-five minutes.

Before he completed construction of a hangar for his collection, John Smith of Mapua in New Zealand, erected temporary covering for his Mosquito to protect it from the weather. *(R. M. Cornwall)*

In 1955 NZ2336 and fifteen other Mosquitos were put up for tender but were withdrawn, and came back on the market in July 1956. John Smith bought NZ2336 and, in order to transport the Mosquito to his home at Mapua, he cut the wing into three sections and also the fuselage behind the wings' trailing edge. When he got home John reassembled his Mosquito and made good all the rotten areas of plywood and fabric, the result of years of storage. John erected a temporary shelter over his Mosquito and over the years has collected most of the missing parts and even had one of the engines running a few years ago. More recently, John has built a small hangar around his Mossie and has also collected together other airframes, including a P.40, Tiger Moth and Vampire. Altogether, this is a remarkable effort by one man and John is justifiably proud this his Mosquito is the most complete example in New Zealand!

Western Springs, Auckland

The Mosquito on long term rebuild with the Museum of Transport and Technology at Western Springs was initially laid down as an FB.40 at De Havilland Australia's Bankstown factory, but before completion it was modified to trainer standards as a T.43, and allocated the serial number A52-1053. After acceptance by the RAAF on 6th August 1946, the aircraft was put into store until December, when it was sold for £3,000 to New Zealand and was issued to No. 75 Squadron on 1st April 1947 with the new serial of NZ2305. After seeing little service, NZ2305 was sold to a Mr Galpin, a farmer in the south of North Island near the town of Marton.

Surplus Mosquitos were often sold off cheaply and many were used as playthings for their owners' children, or bought for useful items such as wheels. This rather sad-looking T.43 NZ2305, ex-75 Squadron (RNZAF), was sold to a farmer in 1955 and survived until June 1967 when it was recovered by MOTAT, and has been under restoration since. In the picture the wings appear to have been cut off, there are no engines, and the nose has fallen off. *(C. E. D'Arby, via Stuart Howe)*

For some ten years, NZ2305 sat rotting away until discovered by enthusiast d'E. C. Darby. Mr Galpin then kindly donated his Mosquito to the newly formed MOTAT, but when Mr Darby started to dismantle the aircraft, it fell apart! The project of rebuilding the Mosquito was first taken on by Peter Dingwall, under whose guidance the fuselage was rebuilt. Dave Stewart then took over the rebuild. In recent times work had all but stopped on the rebuild due to financial problems, but now work has once more commenced, with the aim of finishing the rebuild of the wings. The rebuild of NZ2305 is a great credit to all those volunteers who have put so much time and effort into the project, and we can look forward to a complete Mosquito on display at Western Springs in the not too distant future.

Wigram

Over the course of many years, Ted Packer had collected together many Mosquito components at his home in Christchurch, his aim being to put together a complete FB.VI.

The basis of Ted's collection was the fuselage of TE863, a Standard Motors-built FB.VI which, apart from a brief stay with the Central Flying School at Hullavington, remained in store with No. 27 MU at Shawbury. Sold to New Zealand, it was allocated the serial number NZ2355 on arrival and joined No. 75 Squadron at Ohakea, although, in common with many other Mosquitos, it was shortly afterwards put into storage at Woodbourne and was sold off. Ted later recovered the fuselage and other components from a farm. Over the course of time, Ted also recovered the forward fuselage of TE861 (NZ2324) plus another. Wing parts came from RF597, which had previously seen service with No. 235 Squadron, Coastal Command. Other parts continued to filter through and these included a pair of ailerons from a farm near Woodbourne, one of which still had its D-Day markings painted on it! A pair of Merlins in good condition were also acquired. Over the years Ted collected together two Vampires and many Oxford components, and several years ago donated the latter to the RNZAF Museum.

Due no doubt to time and space problems, Ted donated his store of Mosquito parts to the RNZAF Museum, but did retain one of his cockpit sections which he intends to rebuild. Some seven lorry loads were needed to transfer all of the parts to Wigram!

The author hopes that Ted will eventually work on the restoration of a complete Mosquito, as he is a skilled cabinet maker. It must also be said that if it were not for his fine efforts, the priceless collection he has gathered together would have been scrapped a long time ago.

PR.IX LR480 seen here at San Severo, Italy in 1944. A veteran of many operational missions, this Mosquito is preserved today in Johannesburg, South Africa.
(Ken Smy, via Stuart Howe)

SOUTH AFRICA

Johannesburg

In the South African National Museum of Military History at Saxonwold PR.IX, LR480, is displayed in excellent condition. Hatfield-built in the second half of 1943, it was delivered to Benson on 10th November and soon after was flown to the Middle East. On 8th June 1944 it was issued to No. 60 Squadron SAAF stationed at Foggia in Italy and completed many operational sorties over the Balkans and Austria.

Col. Owen Glynn Davies was instrumental in getting No. 60 Squadron equipped with Mosquitos, and all his Mosquitos were inscribed 'Lovely Lady' on the starboard side of the nose. For some time, Glynn had been wanting to fly a Mosquito from the Middle East to South Africa to try and break the speed record. Eventually, his wish was granted and he took off from Cairo with Brigadier Hingeston as his passenger on 14th December 1944. The first stop after six hours flying was Juba, on the Nile. The RAF servicing party was waiting, but the only means of refuelling the Mosquito was by way of four-gallon cans and it proved impossible to fill the bomb bay tank by this method. After a wasted two-and-a-half hours and an empty bomb bay tank, Glynn replanned the flight to land at Kasma for fuel.

Kasma was found without too much difficulty, and in a very short time the Mosquito was back in the air again, but here the weather became much worse, and even climbing to 35,000 feet did not see them clear of the cumulus. After ten hours at that height, Glynn was beginning to feel exhausted. They were unable to get any weather information and for all they knew Pretoria might be clamped in. However, Glynn spotted an airstrip below and decided to land. Que-Que, for this was the name of the landing strip, was only 2,000 feet long and just too short for the game Mosquito. As they came to a stop, the wheels subsided into a shallow trench at the end of the strip, and the flight was over.

The damage was not very great. The undercarriages and propellers were replaced, and the Mosquito was flown back to South Africa and was subsequently donated to the museum at Saxonwold. LR480's tail-plane is not in fact the original one, for while it was under repair this was donated to another Mosquito that had damaged its own tail-plane! LR480 is mounted on stilts above the exhibition area, but is in excellent condition and is much admired by all.

UNITED KINGDOM

Cosford, West Midlands

Displayed in the ever-growing collection of aircraft at Cosford is long-term resident TT.35, TA639. Constructed at Hatfield early in 1945 as a B.35, it was delivered straight into storage with No. 27 MU at Shawbury, where it remained until delivered to Brooklands Aviation Ltd at Sywell for conversion to target tug standards on 19th May

TT.35 TA639 at Cosford, circa 1973. *(Stuart Howe)*

1952. For two years TA639 served first with the Station Flight at Ballykelly and then with the Aldergrove Target Tug Flight. It was then put back into storage once again, first with No. 38 MU at Llandow, and then at Shawbury.

On 24th September 1959 TA639 was delivered to No. 3 CAACU at Exeter, where it soon became involved in towing targets for the Army and Navy gunners. On 9th May 1963 TA639 took part in the 'Official Last Flight' by Mosquitos at Exeter and, after retirement as a target tug, it was flown to the Central Flying School at Little Rissington on 6th June, from where it made the occasional flight. Shortly after its arrival at Little Rissington it was loaned to Mirisch Films Ltd for the film *633 Squadron* at Bovingdon where it was given code 'HT-B' and the serial number HJ682'.

When eventually TA 639 stopped flying it had only 577 hours on the airframe, and it was allocated the instructional airframe number 7806M. On 5th July 1967 TA639 was transferred to the RAF Museum, first of all to their store at Henlow, and then to the Cosford Aerospace Museum near Wolverhampton. It was re-painted in 1987 and is displayed in immaculate condition.

Chester (Hawarden), Cheshire

British Aerospace's T.III, RR299, is a much admired performer at air displays throughout this country and abroad. Built at Hatfield early in 1945, it was delivered to No. 51 OTU at Cranwell on 18th April, but was here for only a short time, as it was delivered first to No. 27 MU at Shawbury and then on 17th October it was flown to the No. 1 Ferry Unit at Pershore to prepare for a journey to the Middle East. The Mosquito arrived in Aden on 27th December to join its unit, thought to be No. 114 Squadron.

T.III RR299 has been flying for 43 years. It is seen here at its Hawarden base, near Chester. *(Stuart Howe)*

After a year, RR299 was flown back to the UK and was put into store, until issued to No. 204 AFT on 9th June 1949. It was damaged here and after repairs was again put into store. On 16th September 1954 the aircraft was issued to the Fighter Training Unit at Benson, but after three months it went into store once again. Shortly after this, it was put into service with the Home Command Examining Unit at White Waltham, and then

T.III RR299 giving her usual spirited display at a Shuttleworth Trust air show during 1978. *(Stuart Howe)*

served for a spell with HQ's Fighter Command Communication Squadron before being issued to No. 3 CAACU at Exeter where it was used for instrument ratings and annual checks on the unit's TT.35 pilots.

The last flight by RR299 under RAF control was on 14th March 1963, after which it went to No. 27 MU at Shawbury for disposal. Unlike many of the other No. 3 CAACU Mosquitos which saw stardom in the making of the film *633 Squadron*, RR299 was instead purchased by Hawker Siddeley Aviation and was ferried to the HS factory at Hawarden by test pilot Pat Fillingham on 2nd September 1963. The aircraft's first C of A was issued on 9th September 1965. By this time the civil registration G-ASKH was allotted to RR299 but it has never actually worn this registration.

From then on, RR299 started on a busy display career and in 1968 took part in the filming of *Mosquito Squadron*. Its 1,000th flight came up on 21st July 1970. For many years the aircraft came under the care of Harry Robins until his retirement in 1983. Since then, Bill Brayshaw has taken over from him and together with Don Chell, carries out all of the maintenance and inspection checks to ensure that this classic aircraft remains airworthy for many years to come. The current pilots are Hawarden-based Chief Test Pilots Tony Craig and John Sadler, and Hatfield-based George Ellis, who all give up their spare time to fly the Mosquito to the appreciation of us all.

Duxford, Cambridgeshire

This well known airfield houses many famous aircraft, including TT.35, TA719. Constructed at Hatfield in June 1945 this Mosquito was delivered into store and was eventually flown to Brooklands Aviation Ltd at Sywell on 9th August 1951 for a short period before going back into store. On 15th August 1953 it was again delivered to Sywell, this time for conversion to target-towing standards, and its first use in this new role was with No. 4 CAACU at Llandow in April 1954. Shortly afterwards, on 30th June, it was delivered to No. 3 CAACU at Exeter.

TA719 was taken out of service in 1961 and was subsequently bought by Peter Thomas, founder of the Skyfame Aircraft Museum at Staverton, although prior to this the aircraft was loaned to Film Aviation Services for the making of *633 Squadron*. Allocated the civil registration G-ASKC, TA719 flew extensively in the film and was given the spurious code letters 'HT-G' and serial number 'HJ898'. At Staverton its flying career continued until it was badly damaged in a landing accident on 27th July 1964, as a result of which the port

TT.35 TA719 outside at Staverton in the early 1970s. *(Stuart Howe)*

Many of the metal components of TA719 had to be rebuilt, and Ron Smouton is seen here pointing out to Ivy Eastmead how he was rebuilding the engine nacelles. *(Stuart Howe)*

wing outboard of the engine was smashed, and the underside and nose of the aircraft suffered much damage, as did the engine nacelles. Temporary repairs were carried out to the fuselage and a dummy wing was mocked up, and in 1968 TA719 again took part in film work, this time for *Mosquito Squadron*. The long-suffering Mosquito endured further indignities when it was used to simulate a crash landing for the film and was damaged by fire in the process. Other parts, such as the cowlings, were stolen before it was recovered back to Staverton.

In 1978 Skyfame was forced out of its home at Staverton and, along with other aircraft of the collection, TA719 moved into the safe keeping of the Imperial War Museum at Duxford. The IWM gave the task of restoring this sadly neglected Mosquito to Ron W. Smouton. Since then, Ron has replaced the dummy port wing, splicing on a new wing built to the manufacturer's original drawings. Ron also repaired the fuselage, tail-plane assembly and engine nacelles, and today this Mosquito is now looking its proud self again! TA719 may not remain at Duxford, for the IWM's present plans call for it to be moved to their South Lambeth museum to form part of a display there, with their Mosquito T.III, TV959, now displayed at South Lambeth, going to Duxford for restoration. (Late news: TA719 has remained at Duxford.)

London, South Lambeth, SE1

At the Imperial War Museum their second Mosquito is displayed in the form of T.III, TV.959. Built at Leavesden in 1945, it was first allocated to No. 13 OTU at Middleton St George on 29th August 1945, where it was coded 'KQ-G'. Its next move was to No. 266 Squadron on 31st October 1946, followed by No. 54 OTU at Eastmore on 24 April 1947, and then on to No. 228 OCU at Leeming on 17th May, where it remained until delivered to No. 22 MU at Silloth on 30th September 1950. From storage it was then issued to No. 204 Advanced Flying School on 15th July 1951, where it suffered some damage and was sent for repair to Brooklands Aviation Ltd at Sywell. After repair it was sent to No. 27 MU at Shawbury on 6th February 1952, from where it was allocated to the Home Command Examining Unit at White Waltham on 15 May. It remained here until moving to No. 49 MU on 20th August 1953. Towards the end of 1954 TV959 returned to Shawbury until December 1955, when it returned once more to White Waltham. After a short period with the HQ's Fighter Command Communications Squadron, the aircraft joined its final unit, No. 3 CAACU at Exeter on 30th April 1959, coded 'Y', and it was finally Struck Off Charge on 31st May 1963.

Lent to Film Aviation Services, it was used for the cockpit and ground sequences at

Bovingdon for 633 *Squadron*, where it was coded 'HT-P' with the serial 'MM398'. After the filming it was allocated to the Imperial War Museum where it was camouflaged and given the code letters AF-V. In order to fit the Mosquito into its display area, the starboad wing was removed inboard of the engine, and the aircraft was suspended from the ceiling. This work was carried out by a team from No. 71 MU, Bicester. The wing is in store at Duxford, but with the prospect of TV959 soon being replaced by TA719, it will not be long before the wing is mated back onto the rest of the aircraft. Incidentally, the wing at Duxford was recently tested by British Aerospace for evidence of glue separation, but none was found. During an annual inspection the CAA required that part of the wing of RR299 be tested for any sign of glue failure, but rather than cut holes in a perfectly airworthy aircraft, the CAA agreed to test the wing of TV959, as it was manufactured at the same time as RR299's! It was then completely restored by BAe before they returned the wing to Duxford. (Late news: The whole of TV959 is now in store at Duxford.)

London, Hendon, NW4

The Royal Air Force Museum would not be the same without an example of the Mosquito to display to its many visitors and doing the honours here is T.III, TW117. Leavesden-built early in 1946, it was delivered to No. 15 MU at Wroughton on 30th May 1946, and was then allocated to No. 2 Armament Practice Station at Acklington on 22nd July 1947. In 1949 it was transferred to the Station Flight at Linton-on-Ouse where it was used to train crews onto the Hornet and was coded MS-A. On 31st July 1951 it was moved to No. 204 Advanced Flying School. After this the next move was to join No. 58 Squadron at Benson on 28th February 1953, where it was coded 'OT'. When the squadron re-equipped the aircraft was put into storage with No. 48 MU at Hawarden on 30th April 1954. After spells at No. 5 MU Kemble and No. 27 MU Shawbury, it was delivered to No. 3 CAACU at Exeter on 31st March 1960, coded 'Z', and was finally retired on 31st May 1963. Its flying career had not finished, however, for it was lent to Film Aviation Services for the film 633 *Squadron*, where it wore the code 'HT-M' and serial 'HR115'. After filming, it was allocated to the RAF Museum and stored at their Henlow depot. In 1972, prior to its move to Hendon for the opening of the museum, the aircraft was sprayed silver to represent its earlier training days. In April 1983 the Bomber Command Museum opened at Hendon and as the museum's two other Mosquitos, which were both bomber versions, were not available, TW117 was moved a few yards into the new

T.III TW117 seen here in the RAF Museum, Hendon, before it was moved to the Bomber Command Museum. *(Stuart Howe)*

Museum to represent the considerable part played by the Mosquito in Bomber Command. It could well be that one day TW117 will be replaced with one of the bomber variants, but until then this immaculate aircraft remains much admired by all.

London Colney, Hertfordshire

Just fifteen miles north of London, in the grounds of the ancient manor house of Salisbury Hall, is Britain's oldest aircraft museum, the Mosquito Aircraft Museum. Not only is the museum unique in being devoted to preserving a particular aircraft type, but it also strives to keep alive the name of de Havilland, perhaps the most famous of all of Britain's aircraft pioneers. The Mosquito Aircraft Museum is a Mecca for Mosquito enthusiasts from all over the world, and in addition it displays many other de Havilland designs.

Prototype, W4050

Constructed at Salisbury Hall, W4050 (originally wearing Class B markings of E0234) was dismantled and taken by road to Hatfield on 3rd November 1940, just over a year after the Mosquito design team moved into Salisbury Hall from nearby Hatfield. After re-assembly, initial engine runs were made on 19th November, and the first taxi tests were made five days later. After a short hop it took to the air on 25th November at 3.45 p.m. in the hands of Geoffrey de Havilland, with John E. Walker as observer.

The Mossie that started it all — W4050 — being erected at Salisbury Hall in 1958. Standing in front of the wing spar with his hand on the fuselage is the MAM's founder, Walter J. Goldsmith. *(via Stuart Howe)*

After completing thirty-five hours of preliminary manufacturer's trials, the aircraft was delivered to the Aeroplane and Armament Experimental Establishment at Boscombe Down on 19th February 1941 for official service trials. Large 'P' markings were applied to either side of the fuselage just aft of the roundels, this being the standard marking which denoted all prototype service aircraft of the period. Alan Wheeler was the first pilot at Boscombe Down to fly W4050 and he was later to recount: 'My impression of the aeroplane then, and indeed the impression of everyone who flew it, was that it was certainly one of the war winners.'

On 24th February, the trials were brought to an abrupt halt when the tail wheel jammed in a rut and fractured the fuselage just behind the wing's trailing edge. Fred Plumb, de Havilland's Chief Engineer, decided to replace the fuselage with that destined for the prototype Photographic Reconnaissance Mosquito, W.4051, and W4050 was flying

155

again by 14th March. The 100th flight came up on 14th April 1941, during which a speed of 392 m.ph. was attained, and after the successful completion of the trials W4050 returned to Hatfield on 23rd May. Further tests were carried out by de Havilland, and these included investigating stalls and the effects of flying with the bomb doors open, and flying with a mock-up turret aft of the cockpit. Several engine changes were also made and in November 1942 W4050 was flown at 437 mp.h. by John de Havilland, the highest speed obtained by a Mosquito to date. W4050 then went on to complete further engine and propeller tests, as well as other manufacturer's trials, which included the testing of several different exhaust types.

After its flying career came to an end, W4050 was used by the de Havilland Apprentices to practise on. In 1945, it took part in the *Mosquito Story*, the famous film made by de Havilland on the development, production and use of the Mosquito, and in 1946 it moved back to Salisbury Hall, this time for use by the de Havilland Aeronautical Technical School. It also appeared at the 1946 and 1947 SBAC shows at Radlett.

As early as 1945, W. J. S. (Bill) Baird, who was the assistant Public Relations Manager at Hatfield, became aware of the historical significance of W4050, and out of sheer determination was to save it from being burned when after the war it was ordered to be destroyed. To keep it out of sight, Bill had it kept dismantled at Panshanger, then for a short while at Hatfield until he again had it moved, this time to the factory at Chester. When lack of space at Chester eventually meant that W4050 had to be removed, it came back down to Hatfield where it was stored just off the airfield in a hangar known as the Fiddle Bridge Stores.

Meanwhile, a retired Army officer, Walter J. Goldsmith, had bought the by now derelict Salisbury Hall. When he started to restore his new home, he realised that fifteen years before it had been the birthplace of the Mosquito, so he asked if W4050 could go on display in the grounds. This was a relief to Bill, and in order to raise the funds needed to house the prototype, an Appeal was set up. This was quickly raised and W4050 was officially installed at its birthplace on 15th May 1959 as a fitting memorial to all those who were connected with the Mosquito. It is today in excellent condition and is surrounded by many items of equipment, photographs and memorabilia. The prototype Mosquito must surely rank as the most historic aircraft in Britain today.

B.35, TA634

Built at Hatfield early in 1945, TA634 was delivered to No. 27 MU at Shawbury on 14th April and remained there in open storage until 22nd February 1952, when it was flown to Brooklands Aviation at Sywell for conversion to target-towing standards. It was then ferried to No. 22 MU at Silloth in Cumberland on 23rd July and stayed there until 31st December 1953, when it was allocated to No. 4 CAACU at Llandow to carry out target towing operations. During 1954, when No. 4 CAACU merged with No. 3 CAACU at Exeter, TA634 remained at Llandow with No. 38 MU, until on 12th March 1956 it was allocated to HQ 2nd Allied Tactical Air Force, and moved to the Armament Practice Station on the island of Sylt, off the north-west coast of Germany, near Denmark.

B.35 TA634 at the Mosquito Aircraft Museum, Salisbury Hall, in the markings of the aircraft flown by Group Captain P. C. Pickard. (*Stuart Howe*)

It returned to the UK on 26th June 1957 and was put into storage by No. 27 MU at Shawbury until September 1959, when it was delivered to No. 3 CAACU at Exeter, coded '53', by which time it had flown 301 hours and had made 238 landings. No. 3 CAACU's Chief Pilot, Harry Ellis, flew TA634 for the first time on 29th October 1959, a three hour thirty minute sortie to the Army's School of Anti-Aircraft Artillery at Manorbier in South Wales, on a live firing exercise. While at Exeter the aircraft was struck by lightning in September 1960. On retirement from the RAF at No. 23 MU Aldergrove in May 1963, TA634 was purchased for £720 by Liverpool Corporation and flown to the City's Speke Airport on 6th November. The original plan to display it at the airport fell through and the aircraft was put into one of the hangars.

In 1968, a sequel to the film *633 Squadron* was planned called *Mosquito Squadron* and TA634 was found to be in good condition. After an overhaul by Doug Bianchi of Personal Plane Services, a Permit to Fly was issued. On 31st May it was allocated the civil registration of G-AWJV and after a short test flight on 17th June, it was flown later the same day to Bovingdon by Neil Williams, where it was camouflaged and given the fictitious code 'HT-G' and serial 'HJ896'. After nearly eight hours flying in the film the aircraft returned to Speke and was donated to the Mosquito Aircraft Museum in 1970. It left for Salisbury Hall under the care of No. 60 MU team on 29th September, where it was re-assembled. On 15th May 1971 it was dedicated as a memorial to Group Captain P. C. Pickard, who led the famous raid on Amiens jail on 18th February 1944. TA634 was recorded as 'EG-F' to represent the Mosquito flown by Pickard, although the serial TA634 was retained.

For the next ten years the aircraft was kept outside on the hardstanding of one of the old hangars and was well maintained by the author and Mr Goldsmith. When the museum's Supporters' Club was formed in 1975, more assistance was available to help on TA634 and the other DH types that were joining the collection. To house all of these aircraft, in particular TA634, a public appeal for funds was launched to build a second, much larger hangar. This was completed in stages as funds allowed, much of the work being carried out by members, and as soon as the roof was placed in position, TA634 was wheeled in. Edward Pitcher supervised the building operation, but particular mention is made of member Ian Rumney who spent many long days laying the brick walls!

Over the years the fabric covering on the Mosquito had become brittle and the author decided that the only course open was to remove the entire fabric covering and to undertake a complete and thorough overhaul of the airframe. Work commenced in the autumn of 1981, members Peter Waxham and Derek Purchase starting first on the repair of the flaps and tailplane, followed by areas of the wing that had suffered some water seepage. By 1983 repairs to the starboard wing and the fuselage had been completed, although here the only real problem area was around the dinghy hatch where the damp had affected the plywood and balsa underneath. This was not an unusual area to be affected, being fairly common even while in service. Later that year, the author, ably

The Mosquito Aircraft Museum's B.35 nearing completion of its refurbishment in 1986.
(Stuart Howe)

assisted by Ian Thirsk, Dave Bray and Alan Brackley, started work on re-fabricing the entire airframe.

By 1985 TA634's airframe was just about finished, and since then work has concentrated on the refurbishment of the many metal components and both engines, and today TA634 is looking more like her old self. This is thanks to the dedicated work of the MAM volunteers who not only actually carried out the work, but helped raise the substantial amount of money needed to purchase materials and the like.

FB.VI, TA122

Although the FB.VI version of the Mosquito was the most widely built (2,718), the museum's third Mosquito is the only example that exists in Europe today. Hatfield-built early in 1945, it was delivered to No. 44 MU at Edzell on 10th March, and after moving to No. 417 ARF, joined the famous No. 605 (County of Warwick) Squadron, flying out to join the squadron at Coxyde in Belgium on 3rd April. This squadron was one of the most famous of all the Mosquito squadrons, operating in the night interdiction role over occupied Europe.

TA122 was allocated to the squadron's Commanding Officer, Wg Cdr Angus Horne, as his own aircraft, who flew it on an air test for the first time on 4th May. That night Angus, with F/O Arthur Tellett as his navigator, took TA122 on its first and only operational sortie, when they were sent out to discourage enemy ground movements in the area of north-east Germany. Operating near the small town of Esens, near Wilhelmshaven, they fired at some lights on the ground, but the sortie was otherwise uneventful.

With the war almost over, Angus and TA122 carried out some fifty hours of training and courier flights to Berlin, and when he was transferred to HQ's 2 Group he took TA122 with him. Meanwhile, No. 605 Squadron had re-formed as No. 4 Squadron and TA122 was officially issued to the squadron on 13th January 1949 at Wahn in West Germany. However, TA122 was clearly there long before this, as navigator John Archbold flew in the aircraft on 10th January on a one hour thirty minute flight practising GCA approaches at Gütersloh.

P/O Iain Dick joined No. 4 Squadron on 20th March 1949 and his first flight in TA122 was on 21st April when he made a thirty-five minute trip to the Butzweilerhof range, where he carried out Steep Glide Attacks — which was virtually dive bombing, the angle of descent being some sixty degrees. In early September, Iain and TA122, plus several other Mosquitos from the squadron, flew to Britain to take part in the Battle of Britain Fly-Past over London, the last time the Mosquito took part in this ceremony. Iain flew TA122 for the last time on 31st May 1950, carrying out Steep Glide Attacks on the Fassberg

The wing being rebuilt for mating to the fuselage of TA122 is seen here being recovered from Kibbutz Beit-Alfa, Israel in 1980. *(via Stuart Howe)*

The fuselage of FB.VI TA122 on its arrival at Salisbury Hall from Holland on 26th February 1978. *(Stuart Howe)*

ranges on a sortie lasting forty-five minutes. The squadron was by now operating from Celle.

Iain Dick recalls that in its latter days TA122 seemed to spend a great deal of time in the workshops and, with the squadron about to re-equip with Vampires, all the Mosquitos flew back to Britain for disposal, but with TA122 remaining behind. Its unserviceability could well have saved it, for it was Struck Off Charge at Celle on 30th June 1950 and was probably tucked away in one of the hangars to await disposal.

In June 1951, TA122 was bought for £15 by Delft Technical University for use in their Aeronautics Department as an instructional airframe. It was bought complete, but minus engines, and was transported to Holland. In 1958, the University's aviation section was moved into a smaller building nearby, which could house only part of their by now large collection of airframes, which included two P.47's, two P.51's, a P.38, a Spitfire and several other Allied and Axis aircraft. The University decided to keep TA122, but could not find room to store the wing, so this was sawn into small sections, some of which were displayed by the fuselage, while others found their way to the RNLAF Museum and the Aviodome Museum at Schiphol. TA122 later went into storage with the RNLAF Museum, ending up at Gilze-Rijen AFB.

The author, having looked after the MAM's Mosquitos for a number of years, decided to try and obtain TA122 for the museum, and in 1974 started to make enquiries. Negotiations were successful and the fuselage of TA122 was generously donated to the Mosquito Aircraft Museum, with particular thanks to the Curator, Gerrit W. Glerum, and was delivered to the MAM on 26th February 1978. Soon after, the author partially restored the fuselage and repainted it in the markings it wore while in service with No. 4 Squadron in 1949, coded 'UP-G'.

Shortly after its arrival, the writer decided to try and find enough components to rebuild TA122 completely. The remains of a Mosquito were located soon after on Kibbutz Beit-Alfa in northern Israel, consisting of a complete wing and many of the metal

FB.VI TA122 taken during the author's restoration in September 1979. Most of the fuselage has been re-covered and her original markings, UP-G of 4 Squadron, applied. The finish is: top half medium sea grey; bottom matt black; codes Royal blue outlined in yellow; serial white. These markings were applied especially for the Battle of Britain Flypast from West Malling in 1949, the last time the Mosquito took part in this event over London, TA122 being one of them. Note that the nose has been left uncovered to let visitors see the actual construction of the Mosquito. *(Stuart Howe)*

components. With thanks to Harry Tapner and Brantford International, El Al kindly offered to transport the wing to England, and on the evening of 26th July 1980, the wing was loaded through the open nose doors of a Boeing 747F. Arriving at Heathrow the following day, the wing was then transported to Salisbury Hall courtesy of Roy Bowles Transport and Tristar Freight. The whole move was made without the MAM paying a penny out of its much-needed funds, and the museum is indebted to all those who made the project possible. Particular mention must be made of the help given by Zohar Ben-Chaim and the author's friend, Ivy E. Eastmead.

While work concentrated on the MAM's B.35 the wing was stored inside, but in the spring of 1985 work commenced on rebuilding the wing under the direction of Colin Ewer, who had helped build Mosquitos in the immediate post-war years at Hatfield. Colin's task was not an easy one, as all of the wing's plywood skins had rotted away, as had the leading and trailing edges. The spars needed repairs in several places, with almost all of the thirty-two ribs requiring repair or replacement. In addition, several feet of the starboard wing and the port wing tip were missing altogether and all four of the underwing tank doors needed major repairs. The spruce stringers, which run spanwise across the wing, had become exposed when the skins rotted away, but were in a reasonable condition and can be used again. With the assistance of Chris Rowe and Derek Purchase and other museum members, Colin has already repaired both spars, replaced the missing spars on the starboard side of the wing, and repaired and re-fitted almost all of the ribs. The metal components have also been removed and refurbished, such as the undercarriage attachments, and these are now back in place. The aim is to complete the rebuild in time to mate it to the fuselage of TA122 for the Mosquito's 50th Anniversary in 1990. It is not an easy task, when winter conditions hamper progress somewhat, but Colin and his team are getting there!

The wing's identity is still a puzzle. On close inspection the wing was found to contain components from several different Mosquitos, but this has been narrowed down to two Mosquitos, TS449 or TW233, both of which were pre-production TR.33's with non-folding wings. Both of these aircraft saw service in the Royal Navy before they were sold to R. A. Short in 1953, and after overhaul were delivered to Israel by Peter Nock from Blackbushe.

Components to complete TA122's rebuild have come from all over the world: instruments from Malta, a cockpit entry door from Canada (care of the Canadian Warplane Heritage), three-quarters of a ton of components from Wayne Bridges in New Zealand. Ted Packer of Christchurch, New Zealand, has really done the museum proud by sending a container full of parts, which included bomb and cannon doors, spinners, two sets of undercarriages and many other parts. A partly sectioned aileron and elevator still existed at Delft Technical University and these were donated to the project thanks to Professor W. D. Verduyn of the University.

When rebuilt, TA122 will be finished in the markings that it wore while in service with No. 4 Squadron. There is still a long way to go before this remarkable project is completed, but thanks to the many hard-working volunteers at the MAM, plus the many individuals and companies that have willingly supported the project, this will become a reality in the not too distant future.

TT.35, TJ118

When compared to most other surviving B/TT.35's, TJ118 did very little travelling. After being constructed at Hatfield as a B.35, it was delivered to No. 27 MU for storage on 7th September 1945 and remained there until flown to Brooklands Aviation for TT conversion in 1952. After the work was completed, it was issued to No. 3 CAACU on 30th September, and stayed with the unit until 31st May 1957, when it was once again put into store with No. 27 MU. On 31st October 1959 it rejoined No. 3 CAACU but was written off in an accident and Struck Off Charge on 18th September 1961. It was kept at Exeter and used for spares, and in 1963 was purchased by Film Aviation Services for use in the film

The cockpit of TT.35 TJ118 that was used for the cockpit scenes in *633 Squadron*. Note how the cockpit was sectioned, using clips to hold the sections in place. The starboard section could not be found when Eddy Reynolds rescued the cockpit from Elstree and it is now being restored by the Mosquito Aircraft Museum. *(Stuart Howe)*

633 Squadron and transported to Bovingdon. The cockpit was then cut from the rest of the fuselage and was used to film the interior cockpit sequences. It fulfilled this function in 1968 also for *Mosquito Squadron*.

The cockpit sequences were filmed at the MGM Studios at Elstree and the remainder of the fuselage was dumped amongst the film props at the back of the Studios, together with the remains of RS715. When in 1973 the Studios closed down, the cockpit section of TJ118 was also to join the two fuselages on the dump. However, enthusiast Eddy Reynolds salvaged the cockpit and subsequently donated it to the Mosquito Aircraft Museum, where it is still stored. The fuselage of TJ118 went with Dave Elvidge to his home near Oxford to join several other Mosquito components that he had already gathered together. In recent times the fuselage has joined the Oxfordshire Aircraft Collection, whose volunteers are attempting to put together a complete Mosquito. Meanwhile, the fuselage of RS715 travelled north to Huntington with Tony Agar to form the basis of his rebuild (see under York).

The Mosquito Aircraft Museum is open to the public from Easter to the end of October on Sundays and Bank Holiday Mondays, and from July to the end of September on Thursday afternoons. Visits at other times can be arranged and there is also an annual open day and air display. Please contact MAM, Box 107, St Albans, Herts. The museum is situated near the village of London Colney and is just off Exit 22 on the M25 motorway. Tel: 0727 22051.

St Athan, South Wales

At the time of writing, B.35 TJ138 is in the capable hands of volunteers at RAF St Athan undergoing a major refurbishment. Built at Hatfield in 1945, it was delivered straight into store at No. 27 MU and remained there for five years until delivered to No. 98 Squadron at Celle in West Germany on 31st October 1950, where it was coded 'VO'. However, it was back in the UK with No. 38 MU on 28th February 1951 and on 15th July 1953 it was flown to Brooklands Aviation at Sywell for conversion to target-towing standards. The conversion work was carried out by 7th January 1954 and it was allocated to No. 5

Stored for the RAF Museum at Swinderby in Yorkshire is TT.35 TJ138. The photo was taken while in service at Woodvale in March 1958. *(via Isabel Deane)*

CAACU on 16th March, via No. 22 MU at Silloth on 31st January. Finally, it was once again delivered to No. 27 MU at Shawbury on 15th June 1959 and was declared 'Non-Effective' on 5th July. Later that month it was handed over to No. 71 MU at Bicester where it gained the instructional airframe number 7607M. It was used for exhibition and recruiting purposes, one of its outings being part of an exhibition of aircraft at Horse Guards Parade, London, in 1960, resplendent in its No. 98 Squadron markings.

TJ138 was then handed over to the RAF Museum as part of the Colerne collection. When that station closed down it moved to Finningly and then on to Swinderby, where it was used as a backdrop to parades for the School of Recruiting based here. Over the years it was well looked after, but in 1987 it was moved to St Athan for a well deserved refurbishment. After this work has been carried out it is not yet known if this Mosquito will return to Swinderby. It could well go to the Battle of Britain Memorial Flight as a static exhibit, or perhaps replace the T.III in the Bomber Command Museum at Hendon.

York, Yorkshire

Just outside York, at Huntington, Tony Agar has been carrying out a most remarkable rebuild. It all started in 1969 when Tony visited the sites of several Mosquito wrecks looking for small items that he could exhibit. In April 1972 Tony attended the sale of an aircraft collection at Blackpool and there he bought the derelict cockpit section of NF.II, HJ711, and other items, including a rudder. HJ711 served with Nos. 141 and 169 Squadrons, and while with No. 169 Squadron at Little Snoring in Norfolk, HJ711 made the squadron's first 'kill'. This was on the night of 30th January 1944, when the pilot, Sqn Ldr J. A. H. Cooper shot down a Bf 110 near Berlin.

Tony Agar's NF.II HJ711 emerging from his drive-way. *(Tony Agar)*

Tony then decided that he would build a complete Mosquito, and travelled many hundreds of miles collection pieces. He recovered the best parts of a wing from B.XVI, PF498, which had been used by the Civil Defence for crash rescue training at Chorley in Lancashire, and the remains of a wing from a long-derelict Royal Navy T.III, VA878, which had crash-landed at St David's airfield in South Wales. A pair of Merlin engines from NF.30, NT616, were recovered from a Midlands scrapyard, wing tips from Scotland and many more components from all over the country. At this point Tony still lacked a fuselage, but when he salvaged the fuselage of RS715 from the MGM Studios this completed the largest part of the jigsaw. Tony has carried out his work with much skill and determination and it is to be hoped that it will not be too long before HJ711 emerges as a complete aircraft once again.

UNITED STATES OF AMERICA

Dayton, Ohio

The USAF Museum at Dayton has long been trying to acquire an example of the Mosquito for its collection to represent the many Mosquitos flown by the USAAF in World War II and in the closing days of 1984 B.35, RS709, was flown out from England on its way to join the collection.

Built at Christchurch early in 1946, it was delivered into storage at No. 15 MU Wroughton and remained there until 30th May 1952, when it was flown to Brooklands Aviation for TT conversion, after which it was delivered to No. 236 OCU on 31st October. In September 1954 it was returned to store, this time with No. 27 MU Shawbury, until it was finally delivered to No. 3 CAACU at Exeter on 7th June 1956 to carry out its role as a target tug, bearing the code '47'. In May 1963 it was declared surplus and was sold to the Mirisch Film Company for the film *633 Squadron*, where it flew as 'HR113', coded 'HT-D/HT-G'. After filming, it was bought by Peter Thomas of the Skyfame Aircraft Museum at Staverton. In 1971 it was sold to Ed Jurist of New York who based it with the Confederate Air Force in Texas as N9797. Although it did not fly again due to engine problems while with the CAF, it was later sold to Yesterday's Air Force at Chino, California. In 1979, RS709 was again sold and flew across the Atlantic to join Doug Arnold at Blackbushe.

TT.35 RS709/N9797 with the Confederate Air Force in Harlingen, Texas. The photo was taken in October 1977 before she flew to Chino. She is now in the USA at Dayton, Ohio.
(Stuart Howe)

RS709 underwent a complete refurbishment at Blackbushe and was put on the UK civil register as G-MOSI. The Mosquito flew next in September 1983 under the control of George Aird and engineer Harry Robins, but by this time it was clear that RS709 had been sold again, this time to the USAF Museum.

After an abortive attempt earlier in the year, George Aird finally got airborne from Blackbushe on 14th October 1984, the first stop being Prestwick, followed by Reykjavik, Iceland, and Narssassuag in Greenland. However, when approaching the Labrador coast, George noticed that the oil pressure had dropped and on landing at Goose Bay the oil filters showed obvious signs of an imminent bearing failure. A replacement Merlin was sent out and fitted, and the delivery flight recommenced on 31st January 1985. After stopping at Hamilton, Ontario, the home of the Canadian Warplane Heritage, G-MOSI was delivered to the USAF Museum. It is perhaps a pity that a flyable Mosquito is now permanently grounded, but it is in honourable retirement and has become a star attraction at the museum. Plans call for the Mosquito to be modified to represent a PR.XVI of the USAAF, in effect meaning the replacement of the bulged bomb bay doors with the flush fitting kind, this being completed in 1989.

Miami, Florida

As this was being written TT.35, RS712, had just been delivered to its owner at Tamiami Airport in Florida. Built by Airspeed at Christchurch as a B.35, it travelled to several MU's and on 30th November 1951 it was delivered to Brooklands Aviation at Sywell for conversion to TT standards. After completion the following May, it was put into storage at No. 27 MU Shawbury until 31st December 1953 when it was issued to No. 1 CAACU at Hornchurch. When this unit closed down, it was again put into store and on 28th February 1958 it was allocated to the 2nd Tactical Air Force and entered service with the TT Flight of the Armament Practice Station located at Schleswigland in north-west Germany towing targets for NATO forces. It soon returned to the UK and was allocated to No. 3 CAACU at Exeter on 30th April where it was given the code letters '50'.

RS712 was retired on 31st May 1953 and, along with its ex-3 CAACU contemporaries, was acquired by Mirisch Films for *633 Squadron*. It was then camouflaged and dummy machine guns were attached to the nose. For the film it wore the serial number 'RF580' and the code letters 'HT-F'. It was then bought by Gp Capt Mahaddie until in September

Neil Williams running up the engines of TT.35 RS712 at West Malling, prior to flying her to Strathallan in October 1975. *(Dick Richardson)*

1972 it was bought by Sir William Roberts for his collection at Strathallan in Perthshire. The runway was short and this meant only the occasional flight was made. In June 1981 RS712 was sold for £100,000 to American collector Kermit Weeks.

In 1984 Harry Robins took over the task of making RS712 airworthy again and on the 21st December George Aird and Harry flew the Mosquito down to Booker airfield and into the care of Personal Plane Services. Harry then carried out further work and early in 1986 RS712 was camouflaged with the code letters 'EG-F' to represent the Mosquito of No.487 Squadron flown by Gp Capt P. C. Pickard during the attack on Amiens prison in 1944. On 29th September George Aird, together with George Stewart as his co-pilot, left RAF Benson on the first leg to Prestwick, although initially they joined up with Mosquito T.III, RR299, for a photo session near its Hawarden base. After twenty-five-and-a-half hours' flying time RS712 landed at Kermit's museum in Florida, where it will be kept in flying trim and will no doubt be seen at many air shows in the USA over the coming years.

Yorba Linda, California

Here, in the safe keeping of ex-US Navy pilot James Merizan, who in 1970 saved the Mosquito from certain destruction, is FB.VI, PZ474. Built at Hatfield early in 1945, PZ474 was delivered to No. 19 MU at St Athan on 19th April, and on 5th May was allocated to No. 80 OTU, followed by No. 132 OTU at East Fortune on 13th June, coded 'GY' and 'AR'. It then went into long term storage with No. 51 MU on 18th February 1946. On 23rd January it was sold to the New Zealand Government and after an overhaul it was flown to the No. 1 Ferry Unit at Pershore in Worcestershire, eventually arriving in New Zealand on 15th April where it was given its new RNZAF serial number of NZ2384. Allocated to No. 75 Squadron, it is unlikely that it saw very much flying before it was put into store, along with many of its contemporaries.

On 6th November 1952, PZ474 and five other Mosquitos were purchased by two Americans and all were put on the civil register for their delivery flights to the USA, PZ474 becoming ZK-BCV and departing for America in February 1955. The New Zealand Government prevented the other five from leaving as they had reason to believe that they were intended for overseas military use. PZ474 was then placed on the US civil register as N9909F. Its subsequent use is not clear, except for the fact that it was used for intelligence-gathering operations by the CIA in South America.

PZ474 ended up at Whiteman Air Park in California and was cancelled from the civil register in December 1970. The abandoned Mosquito began to deteriorate rapidly and the fuselage was cut in two behind the wing. Not before time it was rescued by Jim Merizan who has restored many of the metal components and has gathered together other Mosquito components. Because of his other commitments Jim has not been able to make as much progress as he would like, but he is getting there. The wooden structure is in poor condition and Jim is looking at the use of plastics to help him in the restoration.

Silver Hill, Maryland

At the National Air and Space Museum's store and restoration facility just south of Washington is B.35, TH998. Hatfield-built early in 1945, it was delivered to No. 27 MU for storage until flying to Brooklands Aviation for conversion to TT standards in May·1952. It joined No. 3 CAACU on 30th September and remained with the Unit until delivered to No. 60 MU in 1962 to be prepared for shipment to the USA as a gift to the NASM, and left early in 1963. It has remained in store ever since, awaiting the day when it can go on display in the museum.

This is an outline of the current Mosquito preservation scene. At one end of the scale are some really splendid examples but at the other there are some very poor ones. These last

The National Air and Space Museum's B.35 TH998 in store at Silver Hill, Maryland, USA.
(David Ostrowski)

are all in the hands of dedicated enthusiasts without whom almost half of the 30 examples listed would not exist today. It is encouraging to hope that others still exist, as two have in fact surfaced recently. There are rumours of examples in China, Turkey, Mexico and India. Pieces are certainly still to be found — two front fuselages in Malta, wing sections on an airfield in Holland, nacelles and other pieces with the Confederate Air Force in Texas, a tail piece in a monastery in Italy and more components in Sweden, Norway, Israel, Australia and New Zealand. Several hundred were exported to about ten foreign Air Forces as well as some for civil use, so it can be hoped that a Mosquito or two (or three!) might survive in such countries as China, Czechoslovakia, Dominica and Yugoslavia.

The Author

Stuart Howe might be said to have been born with an interest in Mosquitos. During the war both parents worked with the aircraft: his mother made electrical components at St Albans, while his father was with the Mosquito Repair Organization at Hatfield. His own active interest began in 1970 when he helped Mr Goldsmith to look after the prototype and the TT.35 for the Mosquito Aircraft Museum at Salisbury Hall. In 1980, Stuart joined the RAF Museum as Manager of the very successful RAF Museum Shop but still manages to serve as a Director of the De Havilland Aircraft Museum Trust, which operates the Mosquito Aircraft Museum, and plays an active role in the running of the museum.

The information in this Appendix is as complete as he could collect, but he would be grateful for information on current progress, and for photographs to be sent care of the publishers.

Mark No.	Serial No.	Country	Location	Remarks
Prototype	W4050	UK	London Colney	E0234 Displayed
NF.II	HJ711	UK	Huntington, York	Comp Re-building
T.III	RR299	UK	Chester	G-ASKH Airworthy
T.III	TV959	UK	London, SE1	Displayed
T.III	TW117	UK	London, NW9	Displayed
FB.VI	HR621	Australia	Narellan NSW	Re-building
FB.VI	PZ474	USA	Yorba Linda	Re-building
FB.VI	TA122	UK	London Colney	Re-building Displayed
FB.VI	TE758	New Zealand	Christchurch	Re-building
FB.VI	TE863	New Zealand	Wigram	Stored
FB.VI	TE910	New Zealand	Mapua	Complete Stored
PR.IX	LR480	South Africa	Johannesburg	Displayed
PR.XVI	NS631	Australia	Point Cook	Stored
B.XX	KB336	Canada	Rockcliffe	Displayed
FB.26	KA114	Canada	Surrey, B.C.	Stored
NF.30	RK952	Belgium	Brussels	Displayed
B.35	RS700	Canada	Calgary	Stored
B.35	RS709	USA	Dayton	Displayed
B.35	RS712	USA	Miami	Airworthy
B.35	TA717	Canada	Mission	Stored
B.35	TA634	UK	London Colney	Re-building Displayed
B.35	TA639	UK	Cosford	Displayed
B.35	TA719	UK	Duxford	Re-building
B.35	TH998	USA	Silver Hill	Stored
B.35	TJ118	UK	Lon Coln/Bicester	Re-building
B.35	TJ138	UK	St Athan	Re-building
B.35	VP189	Canada	Edmonton	Stored
B.35	VR796	Canada	Mission	Re-building
PR.41	A52-319	Australia	Sydney	Re-building
T.43	A51-1053	New Zealand	Western Springs	Re-building

Index